MW00991024

# The Israeli-Palestinian Conflict

crisis in the middle east

ISBN 0-13-100150-7

# The Israeli-Palestinian Conflict
## crisis in the middle east

REUTERS

Published by **Prentice Hall**

Library of Congress Cataloging-in-Publication Data

A CIP catalog record for this book can be obtained from the Library of Congress

Publisher: Tim Moore
Executive editor: Jim Boyd
Director of production: Sophie Papanikolaou
Production supervisor: Patti Guerrieri
Marketing manager: Bryan Gambrel
Manufacturing manager: Maura Zaldivar
Editorial assistant: Allyson Kloss
Cover design director: Jerry Votta
Cover designer: Anthony Gemmellaro
Art director: Gail Cocker-Bogusz
Interior design and layout: Meg Van Arsdale

Reuters: Stephen Jukes
Front cover art photographer: Reinhard Krause
Cover photo copyright © 2002 Reuters

In compiling this book, thanks go to many people. At Reuters: Tim Aubry, Doina Chiacu, Steve Crisp, Dave Cutler, Alan Elsner, Mikhail Evstafiev, Mary Gabriel, Howard Goller, Sonya Hepinstall, Timothy Heritage, Gary Hershorn, Jim Hollander, Stephen Jukes, Reinhard Krause, Robert Mahoney, Peter Millership, Corrie Parsonson, Jessica Persson, Nigel Small, Irina Stocker and Dave Viggers.

© 2003 Reuters
Pearson Education, Inc.
Publishing as Prentice Hall PTR
Upper Saddle River, NJ 07458

Prentice Hall books are widely used by corporations and government agencies for training, marketing and resale.

For information regarding corporate and government bulk discounts please contact:
Corporate and Government Sales, (800) 382-3419, or corpsales@pearsontechgroup.com

All rights reserved. No part of this book may be reproduced, in any form or by any means, without permission in writing from the publisher.

Printed in the United States of America

10 9 8 7 6 5 4 3 2

ISBN 0-13-100150-7

Pearson Education LTD.
Pearson Education Australia PTY, Limited
Pearson Education Singapore, Pte. Ltd.
Pearson Education North Asia Ltd.
Pearson Education Canada, Ltd.
Pearson Educación de Mexico, S.A. de C.V.
Pearson Education—Japan
Pearson Education Malaysia, Pte. Ltd.

We dedicate this book to the courage and commitment
of Reuters colleagues, past and present,
who have covered the crisis in the Middle East.

# Contents

# The Israeli-Palestinian Conflict

crisis in the middle east

Reinhard Krause

# In History's Grip

## Paul Holmes

*"Abraham accepted Ephron's terms; he weighed out to him the silver that Ephron had stipulated in the hearing of the Hittites, four hundred shekels of silver at the current market value."*

Genesis 23:16

Few places are as redolent with history as the city of Hebron in the West Bank, and there are fewer still where past and present collide quite so violently today.

The burial place of the biblical patriarch Abraham, the common forefather of Jews and Muslims, the ancient city is a crucible of the Israeli-Palestinian conflict, a place in which age-old hatreds stoked by religious fervor, politics, prejudice and myth have exploded into horrendous carnage twice in the past troubled century.

It is just a short walk from the home of David Wilder to the home of Abu Samir al-Sharabati in the Israeli-occupied heart of Hebron, a maze of seething animosities where violence between Arab and Jew fills the air. But distance in Hebron is not measured in yards. It is measured in time and it stretches for millennia.

Wilder is an American-born spokesman for the few hundred ultranationalist religious Jewish settlers who live under heavy Israeli army guard in the center of the city, home to some 120,000 Palestinians. His neighbor Sharabati, a Palestinian Muslim merchant, lives with his extended family in an old stone house just beyond the razor wire behind the Avraham Avinu (Abraham our Father) settlement.

Wilder will tell you how the 400 shekels of silver that the Book of Genesis records Abraham as having paid for a family burial plot some 4,000 years ago documents the first real estate transaction by the nomadic Hebrew tribes in the land God promised to Abraham's descendants. That, he says, makes Hebron Jewish soil, the cradle of the Land of Israel.

Sharabati will trace his roots back even farther, citing as his forebears the pagan Canaanites who sold Abraham the very same land. And that, he says, means an uninterrupted Arab presence and makes Wilder and his fellow settlers interlopers.

"There's no love lost between this community and the family there," Wilder told me when I asked him about the Sharabati family during a visit to Hebron late in 2001. "If that property was under Israeli control, it would of course be preferable to the way it is today."

It was not always like that in Hebron, where tradition says Abraham, his son Isaac and grandson Jacob lie buried with their wives Sarah, Rebecca and Leah, in the subterranean Cave of Machpelah.

To Jews who trace their lineage to Abraham through his second son Isaac, the fortresslike building with its part-Herodian walls built above the cave is a synagogue, the Tomb of the Patriarchs. To Muslims who trace their lineage to Abraham through his first son Ishmael, it is the Ibrahimi Mosque.

For centuries both communities lived in relative peace. At times the city's Sephardic or Oriental Jews even found common cause with its majority Arabs against harsh Byzantine Christian rulers and invading Crusaders who transformed the shrine into the Church of St. Abraham.

Then, on August 23 and 24, 1929, with riots spreading through British Mandate Palestine over the Zionist-led immigration of increasing numbers of Jews from Europe, an Arab mob armed with clubs, knives and axes ran amok in the city, butchering 67 Jewish men, women and children.

Dozens, even hundreds of Jews were saved by many of their Arab neighbors. When the killing finally ended, the surviving Jews were resettled in Jerusalem's Jewish Quarter, only to be pushed onto the move again in 1948 when that part of the city fell to the Jordanians. Some Jewish families tried to move back to Hebron but were removed by the British authorities in 1936.

"The attack on the Jews of Hebron was born of fear and hatred," the Israeli historian, Tom Segev, writes in his study of the British Mandate, *One Palestine, Complete*. "The Muslims believed the Jews intended to violate the sanctity of Islam, and that the Zionists wanted to dispossess them of their country."

If that was the case in 1929, 12 years after the British Foreign Secretary Arthur James Balfour cast the favor of His Majesty's government on "the establishment in Palestine of a national home for the Jewish people," it has been all the more so since 1967.

The Jews that have come to Hebron and the imposing hills around it since the Israeli conquest of the West Bank in the 1967 war are among the most extremist settlers in the land. They are armed, anti-Arab and determined, at times in defiance of the Israeli authorities, to extend a Jewish presence on land they consider theirs by divine birthright.

On February 25, 1994, one of their number, Brooklyn-born physician Baruch Goldstein, entered the Ibrahimi Mosque in army uniform with a Galil automatic rifle. Acting under the seeming delusion that he was saving the Jews from another slaughter, he shot dead 29 Palestinian worshippers kneeling in prayer. He was bludgeoned to death by survivors.

Israel handed 80 percent of Hebron to Palestinian self-rule in 1997, making it the only city in the West Bank to remain under partial Israeli military occupation in the wake of the Oslo interim peace deals. The settlers intend to keep it that way.

"The creator of the world didn't bring us back here to throw us out again," Wilder said.

---

*This is the lesson of the Holocaust, this and only this: That the existence of the Jewish people is tied to Jewish sovereignty and a Jewish army that rests on the strength of Jewish faith.*

Israeli Prime Minister Benjamin Netanyahu,
Auschwitz-Birkenau, April 23, 1998

---

For several years now, thousands of Israeli high school students have set out for Poland on a unique rite of passage to confront at first hand the horrors of the Holocaust at the sites of the Nazi death camps.

In 1998, the fiftieth anniversary of the foundation of the State of Israel, Benjamin Netanyahu became the first Israeli prime minister to lead a "March of the Living" on the two-mile trail of tears from Auschwitz to the gas chambers of Birkenau.

With the eyes of the world upon him, Netanyahu used the occasion to repeat what has become one of the defining tenets of Israel's identity: that a strong Jewish state with a powerful army is the best safeguard against another Shoah.

That view is a cornerstone of Israel's justification of its right to exist. Yet such was not always the place of the Holocaust in the Israeli psyche.

The Holocaust gave a terrible impetus to the founding of Israel as a haven for a scattered people prey to centuries of persecution and dispersion.

According to Avner Shalev, chairman of the Yad Vashem Holocaust memorial in Jerusalem, more than 47,000 survivors had immigrated to Palestine by 1947, accelerating the influx of Jews that the British Mandate authorities had restricted for so long.

Thousands more followed, with many taking up arms in the war which erupted when the armies of Egypt, Syria, Transjordan, Lebanon and Iraq invaded Israel the day after it proclaimed its existence on May 14, 1948, in the dying hours of the British Mandate.

Yet the reception the survivors received on disembarking from the creaking vessels that disgorged them onto the sands was not always compassionate.

On occasion it was one of scorn from fellow Jews who were engaged in what they saw as their own struggle for survival and devoted to the creation of a new chapter in Jewish history—one in which Jews would not be cast as eternal victims.

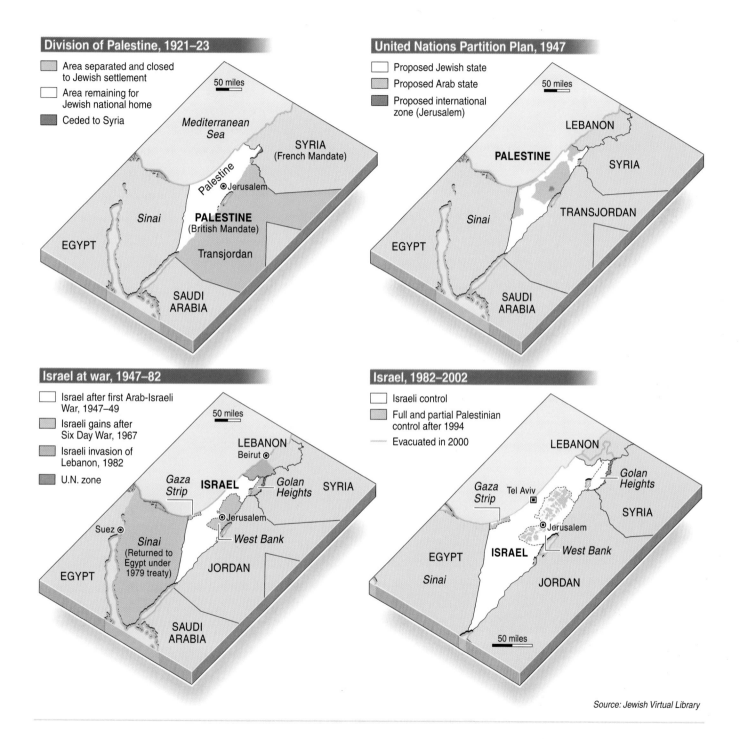

**Division of Palestine, 1921–23**

- Area separated and closed to Jewish settlement
- Area remaining for Jewish national home
- Ceded to Syria

50 miles

Mediterranean Sea

SYRIA (French Mandate)

Palestine

⊙ Jerusalem

Sinai

**PALESTINE** (British Mandate)

EGYPT

Transjordan

SAUDI ARABIA

**United Nations Partition Plan, 1947**

- Proposed Jewish state
- Proposed Arab state
- Proposed international zone (Jerusalem)

50 miles

LEBANON

**PALESTINE**

SYRIA

Sinai

TRANSJORDAN

EGYPT

SAUDI ARABIA

**Israel at war, 1947–82**

- Israel after first Arab-Israeli War, 1947–49
- Israeli gains after Six Day War, 1967
- Israeli invasion of Lebanon, 1982
- U.N. zone

50 miles

LEBANON

Beirut ⊙

Gaza Strip

**ISRAEL**

Golan Heights

SYRIA

Suez ⊙

⊙ Jerusalem

Sinai (Returned to Egypt under 1979 treaty)

West Bank

EGYPT

JORDAN

SAUDI ARABIA

**Israel, 1982–2002**

- Israeli control
- Full and partial Palestinian control after 1994
- Evacuated in 2000

LEBANON

Gaza Strip

Tel Aviv ◼

Golan Heights

⊙ Jerusalem

SYRIA

EGYPT

**ISRAEL**

West Bank

Sinai

JORDAN

50 miles

Source: Jewish Virtual Library

Some in the early years called the newcomers *sabon*—"soap" in Hebrew. It is still slang for "meek" in Israel and a horrific allusion to accounts that the Nazis made soap from the remains of Jews they gassed and burned in Hitler's "Final Solution."

The Holocaust sat uneasily with the pioneering leaders of the Yishuv, the pre-state Jewish community in Palestine, and the young men of the Haganah militia who battled Arab nationalists. For them, with the exception of the rebels of the ghettos and the partisans in the forests, Europe's Jews had gone to their deaths like lambs led to the slaughter.

Zionist logic dictated that the restored Jewish state envisaged by the nineteenth-century founder of modern Zionism, Theodor Herzl, would be a vast "in-gathering of the exiles" who consciously turned their backs on the anti-Semitic oppression and assimilation of the diaspora, not a final refuge born of horror and necessity.

David Ben-Gurion, the Polish-born founder of Israel and its first prime minister, authorized an underground agency to bring Jewish refugees to Palestine, but he also feared that the genocide of Europe's Jews would bring ruin on his Zionist-Socialist design.

"The extermination of European Jewry is a catastrophe for Zionism," Ben-Gurion declared in December 1942. "There won't be anyone to build the country with."

Israeli attitudes toward the Holocaust began to change with the trial of Adolf Eichmann, one of the architects of the "Final Solution." It began in Jerusalem in April 1961 and, for the first time, many Israelis heard witness accounts from victims, some of whom until then had kept the horrors buried deep within themselves.

It was a seminal moment, a national catharsis that confronted Israel's Jews, including Sephardim with no direct experience of the Holocaust, with a trauma that became part of the collective consciousness.

Eichmann, who had been snatched from sanctuary in Argentina and spirited to Israel by agents of the Mossad secret service in a secret operation that became the stuff of legend, was sentenced to death and hanged at the gallows on May 31, 1962.

Menachem Begin, Ben-Gurion's arch political foe from the right-wing Revisionist camp, never shared an ounce of his rival's ambivalence about the Holocaust. From his days when the British put a bounty on his head and branded him a terrorist until his term as Israel's first right-wing prime minister from 1977 to 1983 it haunted his every move.

The first survivor of the Holocaust to lead Israel—his parents perished in Brest-Litovsk—Begin had come to Palestine with the Polish Free Army in 1942. He took command of the hard-line Irgun Zvai Leumi Jewish underground in its fight against British rule, breaking with the mainstream Zionist policy of restraint after the scale of the Holocaust became evident.

Operations he ordered included the bombing of the British military command at the King David Hotel in Jerusalem in July 1946, killing 91 people, and a stunning armed assault in May 1947 on the British-run Ottoman fortress in the Arab town of Acre that sprang imprisoned underground fighters from inside its walls.

As leader of the right-wing opposition Herut party, Begin led vehement protests in the early 1950s against negotiations on reparations with West Germany, declaring in one speech that "every German is a Nazi, every German is a murderer."

Then, driven by the conviction that every Arab threat to Israel held the potential for another genocide, Begin used the Holocaust to justify his policies in government.

"A million and a half children were poisoned by Zyklon gas during the Holocaust. Now Israel's children were about to be poisoned by radioactivity," Begin wrote to U.S. President Ronald Reagan in 1981 in a letter defending Israel's bombing of an Iraqi nuclear reactor. After the massacre of several hundred Palestinians in the Sabra and Chatilla refugee camps in Beirut by Christian Lebanese militias allied to Israel in 1982, Begin said: "Goyim (Gentiles) are killing goyim and the world blames the Jews."

By the late 1970s, according to one study, the Holocaust had come to shape the mindset of all of Israel's Jewish citizens, regardless of their background and culture. It shapes it to this day.

"We have had our Holocaust and we will not repeat it," Gilead Sher, the head of Labor Party Prime Minister Ehud Barak's office, told me early on in the Palestinian uprising, or second Intifada, which broke out in September 2000.

*We sit sometimes and cry over the tile.*

Zuhdia Radwan,
a refugee from the Palestinian village of Deir Yassin

All that Zuhdia Radwan and her husband Mohammad have to remind them of the stone house where they lived as newlyweds is a single decorated floor tile.

They were elderly when we met in their two rented rooms in East Jerusalem's Old City, across town from Deir Yassin, the village on the western outskirts of Jerusalem where they grew up, married and then, as their world fell apart, were turned into refugees.

Half a century on, the core of the old village is now an Israeli mental health center set behind walls as forbidding as the obstacles to a resolution of the fate of the Radwans and millions of other Palestinian refugees.

Shortly before dawn on April 9, 1948, five weeks before the declaration of the State of Israel, Jewish fighters from the Irgun and Lehi underground movements entered Deir Yassin with the reluctant consent of the Haganah.

In the hours of fighting, scores of Palestinian men, including noncombatants, women and children fell to the Jewish fighters in the heat of battle or in cold blood. Accounts at the time spoke of some 250 Palestinian dead, though some Israeli and Palestinian academics now believe that number was greatly inflated.

Deir Yassin remains a pivotal tragedy in what Palestinians call "al Nakba"—the Catastrophe that was the exodus of more than 720,000 Palestinians from cities, towns and villages between November 1947 and September 1949.

Did they flee, panicked by Palestinian nationalists into evacuating their homes or deluded by invading Arab armies into thinking that their absence would last only as long as the imagined "war of annihilation," as official Israel maintains? Or did Jewish militias and the Israel Defense Forces (IDF) terrorize them into flight under a policy to rid the land of its Arab population and make room for more immigrants to the new Israel, as the Palestinians insist?

The reality, like so many aspects of a conflict that feeds off myth almost as much as it rests on historical fact, probably lies somewhere between the two.

"I believe that the Israelis, the Jewish forces, were not motivated in killing Palestinians per se," Sharif Kana'ana, a professor of anthropology at the Palestinian University of

Bir Zeit in the West Bank, told me. "I don't think they really had anything against the Palestinians except that they existed. They wanted them out."

Fighting between Jews and Arabs intensified from November 1947 after Arab rejection of a United Nations plan to partition Palestine into two states with the end of the British Mandate, and the flight of Palestinians continued until the end of the first Arab-Israeli war of 1948–49.

As Israel now reassesses its early years, a group of self-styled "new historians" has arisen to challenge some of the sacred cows of traditional history, including the view that the Palestinian exodus was largely voluntary.

One of those historians, Benny Morris, argues that most refugees fled their homes in the confusion of war, but that their departure also suited Israel and that in numerous cases Jewish and IDF forces intentionally emptied Palestinian villages.

"The memory or vicarious memory of 1948 and the subsequent decades of humiliation and deprivation in the refugee camps would ultimately turn generations of Palestinians into potential or active terrorists and the 'Palestinian problem' into one of the world's most intractable," Morris writes in his study of the issue, "The Birth of the Palestinian Refugee Problem, 1947–1949."

Today, according to the United Nations Relief and Works Agency (UNRWA), there are nearly four million registered Palestinian refugees and their descendants in Jordan, Lebanon and Syria and in teeming, unsanitary camps in the West Bank and Gaza Strip, upon which the passage of time has bestowed an air of underprivileged permanence.

The fate of these families, central to any settlement of the Israeli-Palestinian conflict, poses as daunting a problem today as it did in 1948, when Israel swiftly vowed that it would never allow refugees the "right of return" as expressed in a United Nations General Assembly resolution.

For Israel, the prospect of millions of Palestinians flooding back to cities and towns such as Haifa and Ramle or to villages that now have Hebrew names and Jewish residents is a demographic time bomb that would cancel out its Jewish majority and its reason to exist.

For the Palestinians, a "just solution" to the plight of the refugees is a bedrock principle of their struggle for a righting of perceived wrongs and an issue from which Yasser Arafat derives a strong dose of his legitimacy as the leader of all the Palestinian people.

United States negotiators believed they had devised a way around the problem at talks on a permanent peace settlement at the Camp David presidential retreat in Maryland in July 2000. They were wrong.

Israel, according to published accounts of the outline deal, would grant a limited number of Palestinians a right to return to homes within its borders under "family unification" programs. The remainder would have the option to move to the proposed new state of Palestine, resettle elsewhere or receive compensation for losses to property from an international fund.

Israel balked at the wording and Arafat rejected it, unwilling or unable because of Palestinian and other Arab pressures to compromise on a principle he has termed as "sacred" as the Palestinian claim to Jerusalem.

---

*I took an apple and bit it in front of my men. I told them I had fasted on Yom Kippur since I was 10 years old but now they had to eat and get ready to fight.*

Avigdor Kahalani,
commander of an Israeli tank battalion
on the Golan Heights in the 1973 war

---

It took Israel just six days in 1967 to redraw the map of the Middle East, as much time as the Book of Genesis says it took God to create the world.

Within an hour of the start of the Six-Day War on June 5, 1967, a Monday, Israel had wiped out three-quarters of the Egyptian air force, most of it on the ground.

By the end of the Jewish Sabbath, the territory under Israeli control had tripled in size. Israel gained strategic depth against hostile Arab neighbors with the capture of the Egyptian Sinai Peninsula, the Syrian Golan Heights, the Gaza Strip and the West Bank, and had won the greatest prize of all, East Jerusalem.

After 2,000 years all of Jerusalem was again under Jewish rule. In a heady atmosphere of triumph, secular and religious Jews flocked to the Old City to pray at Judaism's hallowed shrine, the Western Wall, for the first time since East Jerusalem and the rest of the West Bank fell under Jordanian sway in 1948.

Bitter dispute persists over the origins of the conflict, Israel's third in a generation, and whether any of the politicians, Arab or Israeli, had wanted it at all.

But there is little doubt that the Six-Day War had an impact that reverberates to this day through the Middle East and has helped define attitudes to the quest for peace.

Pan-Arab nationalism and the belief of Arab leaders that they alone could speak on behalf of stateless Palestinians withered with the humiliating defeat of Egypt, Syria and Jordan, as did the contention that Israel could be pushed into the sea and wiped from the map.

In Israel, the victory brought a new confidence to the country and gave succor to nationalist and religious movements that swiftly embarked on a settlement drive in the West Bank and Gaza Strip, soil they saw as vital to the security of the state, theirs by biblical heritage, or both.

It immediately posed dilemmas as well—how to handle a potentially hostile population of one million Palestinians, overwhelmingly Muslims, and whether a state that defines itself as both Jewish and democratic should hold onto occupied lands.

Six years later, the deceptive sense of invincibility the victory had bestowed also almost cost Israel its existence.

Avigdor Kahalani was a young lieutenant-general in command of Israel's 77th Armored Battalion at Emek Habakha (The Valley of Tears) on the Golan Heights on October 6, 1973, when he saw a combat aircraft fly overhead.

Kahalani's first question to himself, he recalled more than a quarter century later, was what an Israeli warplane was doing training on Yom Kippur, the Day of Atonement and the holiest day of the Jewish calendar. Then, much like Israel itself, which had seen the signs of a build-up of Arab forces and misread them until it was almost too late, he realized the plane was Syrian and that his country was under attack.

"We knew the facts but we didn't act like we were in danger," Kahalani, whose desperate stand at Emek Habakha helped turn the tide of the war, told me. "We felt like little David against Goliath."

The combined armies of Egypt and Syria caught Israel off guard on Yom Kippur in 1973, storming across the Suez Canal and thrusting deep onto the Golan Heights. Over 18 destructive days, the tank and artillery duels fought on the grass-covered slopes of the Golan and in the sands of the Sinai shook Israel out of its complacency, revived Arab dignity and were to sow the first seeds for peace between Arab and Jew.

"We finished the war 35 kilometers from Damascus and 101 kilometers from Cairo, we had surrounded the Egyptian Third Army, but they had restored their pride," Kahalani recalled.

Before the turn of the decade, Egyptian President Anwar Sadat had done the unthinkable for an Arab leader. He journeyed to Jerusalem to address the Israeli Knesset and then sat down with Prime Minister Begin at Camp David to talk peace.

On March 26, 1979, watched by U.S. President Jimmy Carter, the two men signed a peace treaty at the White House, the first between an Arab country and the Jewish state. It would lead Israel in 1980 to begin a complete withdrawal from the Sinai Peninsula under a "land for peace" formula that remains the bedrock of the unfinished business of an end to conflict in the Middle East.

Their deeds won Sadat and Begin the Nobel Peace Prize, but the treaty would also cost Sadat his life. He was gunned down at a military parade on the eighth anniversary of the 1973 war by Islamic militants opposed to his landmark peacemaking.

By 1982 Israel was back at war, its forces deep inside Lebanon in an invasion masterminded by Defense Minister Ariel Sharon to push the Palestine Liberation Organization (PLO) away from the country's borders and expel its leader, Yasser Arafat, from Beirut.

---

*Before, some of them came here. We ate food together, drank coffee, talked about the situation. I started to give them some trust. I was wrong about that.*

Jamal Haddad, a middle-class Palestinian,
Ramallah, November 2000,
following the collapse of the Oslo peace process with Israel

---

Imagine it is late August 1993 and you are an average Israeli or Palestinian.

Each night for as long as you can remember you have gone to sleep having heard, if you are an Israeli, that Yasser Arafat and his PLO are a bunch of terrorists who are out to destroy your country.

If you are a Palestinian, you have heard that the Israeli soldiers occupying your towns and cities in the West Bank and Gaza Strip are the face of a nation that has usurped your right to historic Palestine.

Then one morning you wake up and hear that Israel and the PLO, through eight months and 14 rounds of clandestine negotiations in faraway Norway, have struck a deal to end decades of mutual hostility, recognize each other and implement a self-rule accord for Palestinians that is designed to lead to a permanent peace settlement.

The Oslo interim peace deal was signed on the White House South Lawn on September 13, 1993, in the smiling presence of President Bill Clinton and sealed with a previously unimaginable handshake between Arafat and Israeli Prime Minister Yitzhak Rabin.

"The children of Abraham, the descendants of Isaac and Ishmael, have embarked together on a bold journey," Clinton told a ceremony that seemed to crackle with all the hope and optimism of an end to a century of conflict between Arab and Jew. "Together, today, with all our hearts and all our souls, we bid them Shalom, Salaam, Peace."

Arafat and Rabin both needed Oslo—the former to restore his stature after siding disastrously with Iraqi President Saddam Hussein in the 1991 Gulf War, the latter to obtain an end to a Palestinian uprising that broke out in 1987. It had brought Israel face-to-face with the dilemma of occupation, and the military force used to fight it was tearing at the country's soul.

Yet the accord struck two unprepared peoples like a thunderbolt. It unleashed fierce internal opposition to leaders branded traitors by critics opposed to the historic compromises it entailed, and it created in those who lived its realities a grindingly depressing sense that the accord was fatally flawed.

What Oslo did not do was create trust, the essential ingredient of the step-by-step approach on which the process was based. It was meant to instill the confidence needed by the two parties to resolve the most difficult problems of their conflict: the status of Jerusalem, the borders of a Palestinian state, the future of Jewish settlements and the fate of Palestinian refugees. Instead, with each side accusing the other of reneging on commitments, Oslo engendered suspicion.

Palestinians ended their uprising and in return got a measure of control over their own lives as Israel slowly handed over towns, cities and villages in the West Bank and Gaza Strip to varying degrees of self-rule.

Arafat, from a lifetime in exile, returned in triumph to lead a Palestinian Authority with the symbolic trappings of a government but none of the powers of the independent state he and his people had believed would follow.

No Palestinian could enter or leave the West Bank and Gaza without passing through one or more Israeli checkpoints. As deadlines slipped and slipped for the implementation of Israeli land transfers, and as Jewish settlements expanded, Palestinians began asking themselves whether they had been hoodwinked.

Israelis were asking themselves the same question. For those who supported the deal, the trade-off was essentially one of giving up occupied land in return for an end to Palestinian attacks on Israeli targets at home and abroad and, ultimately, peace with and acceptance by the wider Arab world. They got neither.

Oslo paved the way for a full peace treaty with Jordan in 1994, Israel's second with an Arab state, but not with Syria or Lebanon, still technically at war with the Jewish state.

Instead of security, Israelis got suicide bombings and shootings from the Muslim militant groups Hamas and Islamic Jihad, Palestinian opposition movements that rejected Israel's existence and whose activities Arafat was either unable or unwilling to control. In short, Israelis did not trust Arafat.

Rabin, like Sadat, paid for his peace deal with his life. As he left a peace rally in Tel Aviv on the night of November 4, 1995, he was shot dead by Yigal Amir, a young Jewish extremist opposed to his concessions to the Palestinians.

In May the following year, disillusioned and traumatized by a succession of suicide attacks, Israelis rejected Rabin's interim successor Shimon Peres, a champion of Oslo, and narrowly elected right-winger Benjamin Netanyahu, one of its most vociferous opponents.

By September 2000, more than a year after the Oslo process was meant to have ended in a final resolution of the conflict, the agreement was a dead letter.

**1250BC**

Israelites begin to conquer land
of Canaan in biblical times

**165BC**

Reconsecration of Second Temple
heralds last independent Jewish
state of ancient times

**63BC**

Romans conquer Jerusalem and
annex Judea (Palestine)

**1516–1917**

Ottoman (Turkish) Empire
rules over Palestine

**1882**

First wave of mass Zionist
immigration to Palestine

**1897**

First Zionist Congress sets aim of
creating a home in Palestine for Jews

**1917**

Balfour Declaration commits to a
"national home for the Jewish people"

**1947**

United Nations votes to divide
Palestine into Jewish and Arab
states. Arabs reject the vote

**1948** May 14

Israel proclaimed. Palestinians
call it al-Nakba (the Catastrophe)

May 15

Five Arab armies – Jordan, Egypt,
Lebanon, Syria and Iraq – attack Israel
and are eventually repulsed

**1949**

Israel wins the war and the territory.
Hundreds of thousands of Palestinians
flee or are forced out

**1969**

Yasser Arafat becomes
PLO chairman

**1969–70**

War of attrition between
Israel and Egypt

**1970** September

Thousands killed in battles
between Jordanian army and
Palestinian commandos

**1971**

Black September group, named after
events of previous year, assassinates
Jordan's Prime Minister Wasfi al-Tal

**1975**

Civil war in Lebanon, Muslims and Christians carry out tit-for-tat
massacres. South becomes battleground between Israel and PLO.
Syrian troops enter Lebanon

**1976**

Israeli raid on Uganda's Entebbe airport
frees hostages hijacked by PFLP

**1977–79**

Egypt's President Anwar Sadat visits Israel.
Camp David Accords – Israel and Egypt
peace. Treaty signed at the White House

**1993**

Oslo Accords sealed with historic White House handshake –
Israeli Prime Minister Yitzhak Rabin and Arafat with U.S.
President Bill Clinton looking on

**1994** May

Birth of Palestinian Authority

December

Rabin, Arafat and Israeli Foreign Minister
Shimon Peres receive Nobel Peace Prize

**1999** September

Israel's new Prime Minister
Ehud Barak signs second
Wye River agreement

**2000** May

Israeli withdrawal
from Lebanon

September

Israel's right-wing Likud party chief Ariel Sharon tours Jerusalem's Temple Mount,
a site holy to Muslims who know it as Haram al-Sharif. Palestinian protests swiftly
escalate into second Intifada

## AD132–135
Attempted Jewish revolt. Destruction of Jerusalem and the Jews as a nation in Judea

## 638
Muslims capture Jerusalem and rest of Palestine

## 1099
First Crusade captures Jerusalem, Muslims and Jews massacred

## 1187
Muslim commander Saladin recaptures Jerusalem and takes possession of Palestine

## 1920
Creation of British Mandate of Palestine

## 1929–36
Arabs stage uprisings against British rule, attack Jewish communities

## 1945–48
Violence rises, Zionist militants blow up British headquarters at King David Hotel and kill U.N. mediator. British block immigration to Holocaust survivors. Arab-Jewish violence intensifies

## 1956
Suez crisis. Israel occupies Sinai but retreats under U.S. pressure

## 1964
Formation of Palestine Liberation Organization (PLO)

## 1967
Israel wins Six-Day War. U.N. Security Council passes Resolution 242

## 1968
Popular Front for the Liberation of Palestine (PFLP) carries out first of many hijackings

## 1972
Munich Olympics: 11 Israeli athletes killed in Palestinian militant attack

## 1973 October
Yom Kippur War. Egypt and Syria attack Israel but are driven back after initial successes

## 1973–74
Saudi-led oil embargo

## 1974
Arafat's first appearance at the U.N. bearing "an olive branch and a freedom fighter's gun"

## 1981
Assassination of Sadat

## 1982
Israel invades Lebanon, occupies Beirut. PLO forced to Tunis

## 1987–93
First Intifada

## 1991
Gulf War – Arafat sides with Iraq. Madrid Peace Conference

## 1995
Rabin assassinated by Jewish extremist

## 1996
Arafat elected president of Palestinian Authority. Hamas suicide bomb attacks

## 1998
Wye River Accords signed by Arafat and Israel's Benjamin Netanyahu

## 1999 May
Fall of Netanyahu

## December
Barak resigns

## 2001 February
Sharon elected prime minister

## 2001–02
Suicide bomb attacks prompt Israeli air strikes and incursions amid U.S. efforts to calm violence

## 2002 May
Arafat free to leave his Ramallah headquarters after month-long siege

David Ben-Gurion makes the historic
1948 declaration of Israeli statehood in
Tel Aviv.

Israeli Government Press Office

Jewish refugees crowd aboard a ship approaching Haifa weeks before the declaration of the State of Israel. Many such vessels crowded with Holocaust survivors were turned away by British authorities.

Israeli Government Press Office

Israeli Government Press Office

Palestinian refugees flee their homes, some five months after the State of Israel was set up.

Israeli soldiers at the Western Wall, June 1967.

David Rubinger—via Israeli Government Press Office

Israeli soldiers clean their weapons in Sinai, 1956.

Israeli Government Press Office

Wrecked Egyptian armor after being bombed by Israeli forces in the Sinai during the 1967 Six-Day War.

Israeli Government Press Office

Yannis Behrakis

A Palestinian mourner walks behind a Palestinian flag, November 12, 2000.

Natalie Behring

An Israeli flag carried by chanting Israeli settlers as they march in a demonstration
close to the West Bank village of Beit Jala, January 7, 2001.

Israeli Government Press Office

U.S. President Jimmy Carter smiles as Israeli Prime Minister Menachem Begin and Egyptian leader Anwar Sadat shake hands after the signing of a peace treaty at the White House, March 26, 1979.

Gary Hershorn

U.S. President Bill Clinton brings Israeli Prime Minister Yitzhak Rabin and PLO
Chairman Yasser Arafat together for a historic handshake after the signing of the
Israeli-PLO peace accord at the White House, September 13, 1993.

**Barbara Kinney, September 1995**

September 28, 1995, is seared in my memory as the most amazing day I experienced in six years as a photographer covering the White House. It was all down to men's ties.

President Bill Clinton was hosting a ceremony at the White House, bringing together Middle East leaders to sign a landmark peace agreement.

One by one, each arrived to greet the president—Israeli Prime Minister Yitzhak Rabin, Palestinian leader Yasser Arafat, Egyptian President Hosni Mubarak and Jordan's King Hussein. Everyone knew this was an important gathering—we were all aware we were witnessing a moment in history.

I spent the next hours taking pictures as they met in the Oval Office. As quietly as possible I recorded the meetings with my Leica. There was an extraordinary photograph to take wherever I looked. Finally, the event was about to begin. I was looking at the group through my lens with my right eye, focusing on the President.

It was then that Stephen Goodin, the President's personal aide, said "Mr. President— you need to straighten your tie." In the blink of an eye, the other leaders began to check their neckties as well. I snatched three quick frames before the scene broke up.

I was well aware that this intimate moment would make a great picture but had doubts whether in my haste it was in focus. To my enormous relief later that day, my picture editor congratulated me that indeed it was an amazing photograph and it was in focus.

It won first place in the "People in the News" category at the World Press Photo Foundation ceremony in Amsterdam in April 1996.

Barbara Kinney

Jim Hollander

U.S. President Bill Clinton applauds Israeli Prime Minister Yitzhak Rabin (left) and Jordan's King Hussein after a peace treaty signing ceremony held along the desert border north of Aqaba and Eilat on October 26, 1994.

Israeli Prime Minister Benjamin
Netanyahu looks at Palestinian leader
Yasser Arafat at the White House in
Washington during the emergency
Middle East Peace Summit,
October 1–2, 1996.

Stephen Jaffe

Win McNamee

World leaders watch as the coffin of assassinated Israeli Prime Minister Yitzhak Rabin is placed on a stand during funeral services in Jerusalem, November 6, 1995. From left are German Chancellor Helmut Kohl, German President Roman Herzog, United Nations Secretary-General Boutros Boutros Ghali, Egyptian President Hosni Mubarak, U.S. President Bill Clinton, Dutch Prime Minister Wim Kok, Dutch Queen Beatrix, and acting Israeli Prime Minister Shimon Peres.

Desmond Boylan

A Palestinian woman walks past a bloodied hand print left after the death of 16-year-old Palestinian Samir Ammar al-Mashni in Jerusalem's Old City on December 8, 2000. Mashni was shot and killed after fighting broke out between Palestinian stone throwers and Israeli soldiers and police after Friday prayers near the al-Aqsa Mosque.

A Palestinian boy holds a ball in Jerusalem's Old City as an Israeli soldier stops during a routine patrol in 1988.

Jim Hollander

Jim Hollander

An ultra-Orthodox Jew takes cover between cars on the outskirts of the West Bank city of Nablus as a gunbattle breaks out between Jewish settlers and Palestinians in October 2000.

Magnus Johansson

A Palestinian boy jumps over a tear gas canister during clashes with Israeli soldiers near the West Bank town of Bethlehem, August 31, 2001.

Jewish American Ronit Lorch, 15, places the last candle to form the Star of David, the symbol of the State of Israel, during a vigil on March 9, 1996, in Jerusalem at the site of a bus bombing which had killed 19 people six days earlier.

Yannis Behrakis

Ahmed Jadallah

A Palestinian refugee girl holds onto a pole in a tent in Khan Younis refugee camp in the Gaza Strip, April 24, 2001.

Muslims kneel in prayer in Jerusalem at the start of the holy month of Ramadan, November 16, 2001.

Natalie Behring

A Jewish man prays at the Western Wall surrounded by other worshippers covered in white prayer shawls as thousands gather for a special prayer in honor of the Jewish holiday of Passover, April 10, 2001.

Security guards at a site where peace activists laid out mock coffins, two of which are covered with Israeli and Palestinian flags, in Tel Aviv, March 13, 2002. The coffins represented 341 Israelis (white coffins) and 1,058 Palestinians (black coffins) who were killed in 18 months of the Palestinian uprising.

Havakuk Levison

# The Second Intifada:
## from the brink of peace
## to the depths of hatred

### Timothy Heritage

It was a time bomb waiting to explode, but for many people it was still a shock when the second Palestinian uprising erupted in September 2000.

Israelis and Palestinians disagree over what pushed them into their worst violence in decades, just two months after Palestinian President Yasser Arafat and Israeli Prime Minister Ehud Barak failed to reach a final peace agreement that would have ended their conflict at the Camp David peace summit. But few would disagree that the outcome left the Israelis and the Palestinians further apart than they had been for many years.

Israelis point to the death of an Israeli soldier in a Palestinian ambush in the Gaza Strip on September 27. Palestinians say the explosion of violence was triggered by a controversial visit the next day by Ariel Sharon, then a right-wing opposition leader, to a holy site in Jerusalem revered by both Muslims and Jews.

Sharon's brief visit to what is known by Jews as Temple Mount and by Muslims as the Haram al-Sharif, or Noble Sanctuary, angered the Palestinians. They said the presence of an Israeli leader in the shadow of the Dome of the Rock and al-Aqsa mosques defiled the third holiest site in Islam. Scuffles broke out between Israeli police guarding Sharon and Muslim protesters.

Tensions mounted as Palestinians flocked to Friday prayers the following day and pitched battles erupted between police and protesters. Police opened fire on the crowd, killing six Palestinians.

The rebellion, which the Palestinians would come to call the al-Aqsa Intifada, was well and truly under way. Many Israelis believe it was well planned in advance and encouraged by Arafat. Palestinian leaders said the revolt was spontaneous and that they were powerless to control anger overflowing after more than three decades of Israeli occupation.

Even then it was not clear that a chain of events had been set in motion that would destroy the trust that had been nurtured during a decade of peacemaking during the 1990s, the era of the Oslo interim peace accords.

By the time Camp David failed, many Palestinians had already lost faith in a peace process that had failed to remove Jewish settlers and soldiers from their midst and had failed to deliver sufficient economic gains for a people, many of whom were still living in refugee camps suffering from grinding poverty and endemic unemployment.

"Palestinians have lost hope in the peace process. There is no hope in the future and they have nothing to lose," Raji Sourani, director of the Palestinian Center for Human Rights in the Gaza Strip, said days after the violence began. Two years later, the Palestinian economy was shattered, hundreds of families had lost loved ones and the infrastructure of what might have been the framework for a Palestinian state lay in ruins.

The uprising rapidly took on a grim momentum of its own. Young Palestinians tied on headbands commando-style before hurling stones and petrol bombs at soldiers in a deadly cat-and-mouse game, just as they had in the first Intifada that lasted from 1987 to 1993. But a deadly difference quickly emerged. This time, some Palestinians were armed with guns as well as stones. And the Palestinians had found a new weapon which struck fear and panic into the hearts of all Israelis—suicide bombers. Most were young men, carefully prepared for their missions, but as time went on, there were isolated cases of women joining the volunteers, strapping explosives to themselves to kill Israelis.

A pattern developed that perpetuated the conflict. Each Palestinian death was followed by a mass funeral that fueled calls for revenge and more violence, which in turn led to more deaths, more funerals and again more violence. Each Palestinian death and each funeral was widely shown on satellite television throughout the Arab world, stirring more fury. Each Israeli death deepened anger among the Israeli population and increased pressure for a tougher military response—which often followed.

For many of the foreign reporters covering the conflict, a strange pattern also developed. This was a war fought almost on their doorstep. In some cases, reporters could travel to the war zone, witness the fighting, and then return to their comfortable homes in Jerusalem. Some found this a disturbing phenomenon, very different from the experience of covering other conflicts such as in the Balkans and Chechnya, where reporters were more likely to spend days or weeks on end trapped in the middle of the fighting. Every reporter has his or her own hair-raising tale to tell—a bullet that narrowly missed or a tank shell that

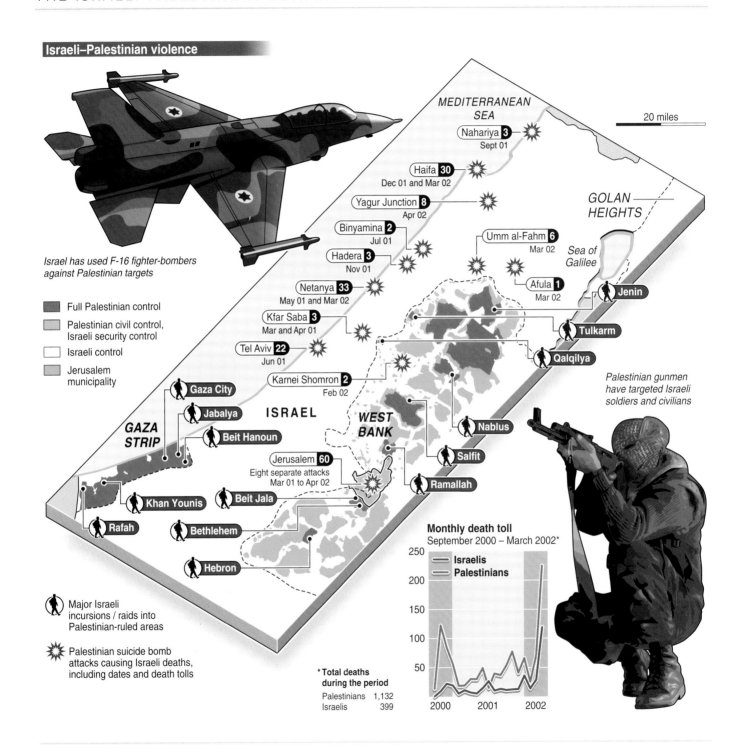

## Israeli–Palestinian violence

Israel has used F-16 fighter-bombers against Palestinian targets

- Full Palestinian control
- Palestinian civil control, Israeli security control
- Israeli control
- Jerusalem municipality

MEDITERRANEAN SEA

20 miles

GOLAN HEIGHTS

Nahariya **3**
Sept 01

Haifa **30**
Dec 01 and Mar 02

Yagur Junction **8**
Apr 02

Binyamina **2**
Jul 01

Hadera **3**
Nov 01

Netanya **33**
May 01 and Mar 02

Kfar Saba **3**
Mar and Apr 01

Tel Aviv **22**
Jun 01

Karnei Shomron **2**
Feb 02

Umm al-Fahm **6**
Mar 02

Sea of Galilee

Afula **1**
Mar 02

Jenin

Tulkarm

Qalqilya

ISRAEL

WEST BANK

Nablus

Salfit

Ramallah

GAZA STRIP

Gaza City
Jabalya
Beit Hanoun
Khan Younis
Rafah

Jerusalem **60**
Eight separate attacks
Mar 01 to Apr 02

Beit Jala
Bethlehem
Hebron

Palestinian gunmen have targeted Israeli soldiers and civilians

Major Israeli incursions / raids into Palestinian-ruled areas

Palestinian suicide bomb attacks causing Israeli deaths, including dates and death tolls

\* Total deaths during the period
Palestinians  1,132
Israelis      399

### Monthly death toll
September 2000 – March 2002\*

- Israelis
- Palestinians

250
200
150
100
50

2000    2001    2002

landed perilously close—but danger could also lurk around the corner closer to home. A suicide bomber blew herself up in my local supermarket. A bomber struck close to my children's school minutes before they arrived.

In the early confrontations, Palestinian protesters armed mainly with stones, some with petrol bombs and a few with guns, confronted well-equipped Israeli soldiers. Many of the dead were Palestinian youths and children, killed as they took turns running out from hiding and lobbing stones at soldiers and their tanks.

Twelve-year-old Mohammad al-Dura quickly came to symbolize the Palestinian struggle. Trapped by gunfire at the Netzarim junction in the Gaza Strip as he and his father made their way home on September 30, they were caught on film crouching behind a concrete barrel in front of a wall as bullets ricocheted around them. The heart-stopping footage showed the youngster's father trying in vain to shield his son, screaming for help and then swaying from side to side with his son's lifeless body slumped across his lap. Posters of the dead boy soon appeared in Palestinian areas. Egypt named a street after him. He became a symbol of the Palestinian uprising, although Israel said there was no evidence its troops killed him.

The Israelis also had their symbols. Two soldiers, trapped in a building in Ramallah, were killed by an angry mob which threw one of the bodies out of a first-floor window. Some of the murderers held up hands literally dripping with blood to be photographed by journalists. An Israeli shrine, said to be the tomb of the biblical Joseph, was overrun and badly damaged by a Palestinian crowd.

In one of the most unforgettable and disturbing moments of the Intifada, the wife of one of the lynched soldiers called him on his mobile phone as he was being killed.

One of his Palestinian attackers took the call. An equally disturbing moment was the killing of the wife of a Palestinian militant in Ramallah and their two children by a tank shell that hit their car as they drove home from school. The mistake was later admitted by the Israeli army. By the time I reached the scene, just minutes later, the first bodies were being taken out of the smoking wreckage. There was blood and flesh splattered across the car, but the lasting memory was of the bloodied school books lying beside the bodies. Similarly, it was often the image of an abandoned child's shoe or an empty stroller among the shattered glass, blood and rubble after a suicide bombing that lingered in the memory.

As the weeks went by, and the death toll mounted, the Palestinians resorted increasingly to new tactics, planting roadside bombs to trap Israeli army convoys, raiding army outposts and Israeli settlements at night in the West Bank and Gaza Strip, and shooting at cars on roads mainly used by Jewish settlers and soldiers.

Israel stepped up its own use of force, carrying out what it called pinpoint operations to kill militant Palestinians whom it accused of carrying out or planning attacks. Palestinians condemned them as assassinations. Israeli helicopter gunships and warplanes were brought into action, launching missile strikes at Palestinian security targets in cities, including Gaza and Ramallah.

As anger mounted, peace hopes receded. International diplomats came and went, launching a series of fruitless efforts to arrange a permanent cease-fire. But every time the parties agreed to a cease-fire, it quickly collapsed or never truly took hold.

Life in the Holy Land, the Promised Land, became far from holy and held out little promise.

There were tragic tales on both sides, and many innocent victims of all ages. Palestinian brothers Bilal and Dilal Salah were shot on October 29, 2000, on the slope of an exposed hillside in Ya'bad in the northern West Bank. "They lived together. They died as two," their mother, Um Zuhair, said as she mourned them.

Five members of the Schijveschuurder family—Mordechai, aged 43, Tzira, 41, Ra'aya, 14, Avraham Yitzhak, 4, and Hemda, 2—were killed in a Palestinian suicide bombing which ripped apart the Sbarro pizzeria in Jerusalem on August 9, 2001.

Palestinians had their olive trees bulldozed and were forced to go through humiliating security checks at Israeli roadblocks that sprung up across the West Bank. Israelis grew fearful about riding a bus or going to a restaurant, or attending a wedding or a bar mitzvah. Death came in many shapes and forms, sometimes when it was least expected.

Disillusioned with Prime Minister Barak's efforts to halt the violence, voters abandoned the center-left prime minister at an election in February 2001 and handed Sharon a landslide victory on a ticket to improve Israelis' security.

The violence intensified. The world looked on aghast but unable or unwilling to intervene as Arafat and Sharon, two old foes, locked horns again. Sharon had refused in the past to shake Arafat's hand and now he ruled out talks under fire. Arafat's own desire for peace was limited by his belief that he could not afford to abandon the uprising without something to show for the bloodshed that had deepened the economic crisis in Palestinian-ruled areas and resulted in a daily rising death toll.

Hopes of American intervention faded with the departure of President Bill Clinton and the arrival of George W. Bush in January 2001. Bush set out to keep his distance from the Middle East peace process and steer clear of the pitfalls his predecessor failed to avoid. By the time Bush did re-engage in the conflict, after launching a global war on terror following the attacks on the United States on September 11, 2001, the violence was already spinning out of control. Critics said the U.S. intervention was too little, too late.

The militant Muslim groups Hamas and Islamic Jihad gradually started to play a bigger role as the uprising dragged on. They eventually unleashed a full-scale campaign of suicide bombings that was joined by the newly formed al-Aqsa Martyrs Brigades, a group with links to Arafat's Fatah movement. The Brigades later took a leading role in the suicide bombing campaign which hit a peak in 2002 after Sharon sent tanks into Palestinian refugee camps on what he said were sweeps for militants.

The suicide attacks hit with increasing ferocity and frequency and left Israelis wondering if they were safe anywhere. In the deadliest attack, a young Palestinian with a bag full of explosives burst into a packed hotel dining room in the coastal city of Netanya on March 27 and blew himself up, killing 29 Israelis as they sat down for the Passover seder, a ceremonial meal at the start of the week-long Jewish holiday that marks the biblical exodus from Egypt.

Sharon responded quickly. He summoned top ministers and ordered the most extensive Israeli military operation in the West Bank and Gaza Strip since Israel seized the territories in the 1967 Middle East war. Troops briefly entered or temporarily reoccupied the main West Bank cities in what Israel called an effort to break "an infrastructure of terror" and surrounded Arafat's West Bank headquarters in the city of Ramallah. One by one tanks took over the towns and searched house-to-house for militants. Men were stripped to the waist and forced to stand with their hands above their heads as they were checked for weapons. Some were blindfolded. Some had their hands tied.

Palestinians at first said hundreds of people were killed in the Jenin refugee camp, the scene of the heaviest fighting, but Israel said the death toll was much lower and denied Palestinian claims that the army had committed a massacre.

Israel said its operation crippled the Palestinians' ability to carry out attacks on Israelis. Many Palestinians said the army had managed only to deepen resentment that would encourage more violence and create new suicide bombers.

It was no surprise when a suicide bomber struck as the Israeli military offensive wound down. Sharon was just sitting down for talks with Bush in Washington on May 7, 2002, when a man walked into a crowded billiard hall south of Tel Aviv and detonated a bomb packed with nails and pieces of metal, killing at least 15 people.

"The will of our people is stronger than the tanks," Mahmoud al-Zahar, a Hamas leader in the Gaza Strip, declared.

At first it seemed that Arafat had emerged from the siege of Ramallah strengthened. This was a man who clearly thrived on adversity. In an interview at the outset of the Intifada in Gaza, he had seemed ill at ease, nervous and unconvincing, somehow a smaller personality than I had expected. Yet in another interview more than a year later during his confinement in Ramallah, he came across as confident and determined. He laughed as he looked out of his office window at the Israeli tanks surrounding him. He chatted jovially over a meal of chicken and rice, passing his guests a plate of his favorite nuts to try.

Yet when the siege ended, Arafat's popularity among his people sank quickly and he faced loud calls for reform. When he visited Jenin, he did not go to the refugee camp. Aides cited security concerns, but some officials privately acknowledged he would have faced criticism of his Palestinian Authority and its security forces. Standing on the rubble of homes flattened by the Israeli onslaught, residents of the camp did not chant Arafat's name as they waited in the scorching heat for him to appear. Instead they chanted the name of a local Islamic Jihad leader who had been killed resisting the Israeli troops. Their main allegiance was not to Arafat, and years of Arafat rule that had brought neither permanent peace nor prosperity had alienated them. Two days later Arafat announced plans to overhaul the Palestinian Authority and hold elections.

After more than a year and a half of bloodshed, there were few signs of hope. United States intervention seemed vital if the two sides were to make peace. But the question being openly asked was whether a deal was possible with Arafat and Sharon in charge.

Nayef Hashlamoun

A Palestinian youth clutches a handful of stones behind his back on a main street in the West Bank city of Hebron during clashes between Palestinian stone throwers and Israeli soldiers, December 12, 2000.

An Israeli tank advances toward a Palestinian youth during clashes near the office of Palestinian leader Yasser Arafat in the West Bank city of Ramallah, February 8, 2002.

Ammar Awad

Osama Silwadi

A Palestinian boy uses a sling to throw a stone at Israeli soldiers during clashes in the West Bank city of Ramallah, January 21, 2002.

An Israeli soldier aims his gun at a Palestinian youth stripped to the waist during Palestinian-Israeli clashes in the southern Gaza Strip town of Khan Younis, October 20, 2000.

Reinhard Krause

Laszlo Balogh

An Israeli tank shell explodes at the headquarters of Palestinian leader Yasser Arafat in the West Bank city of Ramallah as the military takes control of his compound, March 29, 2002.

Laszlo Balogh

Israeli soldiers enter the damaged headquarters of Palestinian President Yasser Arafat
in the West Bank city of Ramallah, March 29, 2002.

A view of the Church of the Nativity from an Israeli forces position in Manger Square, Bethlehem, during an armed stand-off between Israeli forces and Palestinian gunmen, May 2, 2002.

Goran Tomasevic

Oleg Popov

An Israeli army tank takes up position in front of the door of the Church of the
Nativity in Bethlehem, May 9, 2002.

A priest watches as the last group of Palestinians leaves Bethlehem's Church of the Nativity under a deal ending a 38-day armed stand-off at one of Christianity's holiest sites, May 10, 2002.

Gil Cohen Magen

A Palestinian walks behind a half-burned Koran at the military offices in the refugee camp of Deir al-Balah in the Gaza Strip shortly after an Israeli missile struck the building, April 10, 2001.

Damir Sagolj

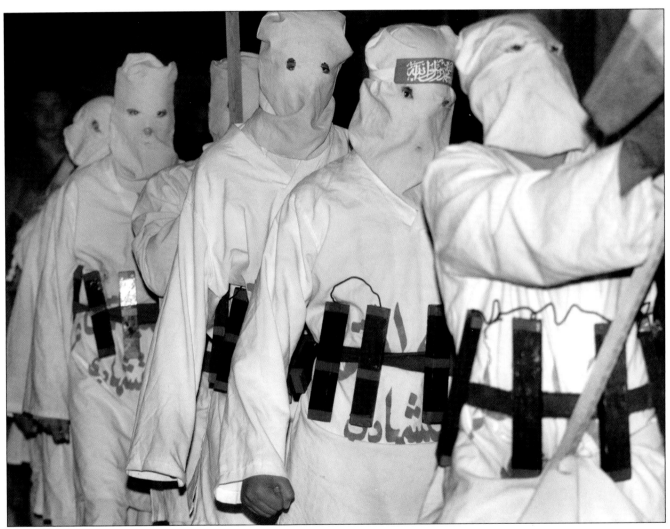

Suhaib Salem

Masked Palestinian members of the Hamas movement, wearing white robes and mock explosives showing they are ready to become suicide bombers, take part in a protest at Jabalya refugee camp in the Gaza Strip supporting suicide attacks inside Israel, March 3, 2002.

Laszlo Balogh

A news photographer captures the destruction at the Park Hotel at the Passover seder dinner, March 27, 2002. A Palestinian suicide bomber attacked the hotel in the Israeli coastal resort town of Netanya, killing 29 Israelis and wounding more than 100 others.

Friends of slain Israeli soldier Amir Mansuri, who was killed in an ambush in the Gaza Strip, mourn during his funeral in Jerusalem, February 19, 2002.

Reinhard Krause

The coffin of Yahya Ayyash is carried into a Palestinian mosque in Gaza City for funeral services as Hamas supporters rush to touch the plain wooden coffin, January 6, 1996. Ayyash, known as "The Engineer," was killed January 5 when a booby-trapped cellular telephone he was using exploded. He was responsible for the death of dozens of Israelis in suicide bombings and topped Israel's most-wanted list.

Jim Hollander

Palestinians try to put out a fire blazing in Palestinian President Yasser Arafat's helicopter that was destroyed during an Israeli missile strike in Gaza, December 3, 2001.

Suhaib Salem

An Israeli police officer stands in front of a burned-out bus and the wreckage of a car after bombs exploded at the busy Beit Lid junction, September 9, 2001. Seventeen Israelis were injured in the blast, which killed the bomber.

Nir Elias

At a rally in Hebron University, December 11, 2000, Palestinian women sit before a mural of portraits of Palestinians killed during the second Intifada.

Loay Abu Haykel

Ammar Awad

A Palestinian woman gestures as Israeli tanks enter a refugee camp near the West
Bank town of Bethlehem, March 10, 2002.

The father of Sofia Eliyahu, 23, and grandfather of seven-month-old Yakov Eliyahu, mourns at his daughter's and his grandson's grave in Noam, March 3, 2002. A Palestinian suicide bomber blew himself up the day before on a crowded street in an ultra-Orthodox neighborhood of Jerusalem as worshippers were leaving synagogues at the end of the Sabbath. Nine people, five of them children, were killed.

Tsafrir Abayov

Nayef Hashlamoun

Palestinian children watch Israeli soldiers during a curfew after Israelis closed the Old City in the West Bank city of Hebron, August 1, 2001.

An Israeli soldier talks
to Palestinian children
at the entrance to the
Old City of the West
Bank town of Hebron
that was under curfew,
February 20, 2002.

Loay Abu Haykel

A Palestinian boy holding a flag ducks as Israeli gunfire breaks out at the Gush Katif Jewish settlement near Khan Younis in the southern Gaza Strip, November 7, 2000.

Jerry Lampen

Abed Omar Qusini

Palestinian boys undergo training during a military-style camp in the West Bank village of Beita near Nablus, August 12, 2001. Some 120 Palestinian youths took part in the ten-day program organized by the Fatah movement.

A masked Palestinian youth walks in front of burning tires during clashes near the Jewish settlement of Netzarim in the Gaza Strip, July 29, 2001.

Suhaib Salem

Laszlo Balogh

Palestinians lie on the ground in front of an Israeli tank after they were arrested during an Israeli operation in the West Bank city of Ramallah, March 30, 2002.

Magnus Johansson

Palestinians lift their shirts to show Israeli forces they have no concealed weapons or explosives in the Dheisheh refugee camp near the West Bank town of Bethlehem, March 11, 2002.

**Reinhard Krause, October 2000**

I vividly remember the panic among these Palestinian youths as they fled to escape a salvo of tear gas canisters and rubber bullets fired by Israeli soldiers. The photo was taken in the Gaza Strip town of Khan Younis, and the soldiers were guarding the Jewish settlement of Gush Katif. A group of young Palestinians hiding behind a sand dune had thrown stones at the soldiers, provoking a response.

As they took off, a youth suddenly appeared in the foreground. The fact that he was scrambling in the other direction seemed strange at the time. I took the frame, but there was no time to think much as I fled from danger. In the coming weeks many Palestinians were injured and some were killed during the clashes that ensued.

After that it escalated into a daily exchange of gunfire between Palestinian gunmen and Israeli soldiers. Most of the Palestinian houses close to the settlement were destroyed by Israeli troops, because the army said they were used as gunmen's positions. The area where the picture was taken became a "No Go Area" where anyone trying to approach the settlement risked an army sniper's bullet. Still several suicide bombers managed to get through and cause carnage.

Reinhard Krause

A Palestinian police officer (left) argues with an Israeli soldier (right) as a settler points his machine gun at another Palestinian police officer during an anti-settlement protest by Palestinians near the Kfar Yam Jewish settlement in the southern Gaza Strip, June 28, 2000.

Suhaib Salem

Palestinians walk in a destroyed area of the Jenin refugee camp, April 25, 2002.

Reinhard Krause

Jerry Lampen

A Palestinian man adjusts the body of a 12-year-old Palestinian boy as he is buried in the southern town of Rafah in the Gaza Strip, December 2, 2000. The boy was killed by Israeli soldiers on December 1 during clashes between Palestinian youths and Israeli soldiers.

Reinhard Krause

The coffin of slain Israeli soldier Ofir Kit is carried at his funeral in Jerusalem, June 24, 2001. Kit and another soldier were killed and a third was injured by a suicide car bomb on a road in the northern Gaza Strip.

Jerry Lampen

A relative of a slain Palestinian youth breaks down in tears after the body arrived at his family home prior to the funeral, November 11, 2000. He was killed by Israeli soldiers at Karni crossing in the Gaza Strip.

Reinhard Krause

A Jewish man mourns at the site where nine Jews were killed the day before by a
Palestinian suicide bomber in an ultra-Othodox Jewish neighborhood of Jerusalem,
March 3, 2002.

Doves and pigeons fly in front of an Israeli tank entering the West Bank town of Tulkarm as Israel pushes its forces into two Palestinian refugee camps, March 7, 2002.

Abed Omar Qusini

A Palestinian youth hurls a petrol bomb at Israeli troops guarding a Jewish settlement in the heart of Hebron, December 12, 1997.

Rula Halawani

A Palestinian boy sits on a staircase stained with blood at a house in the Jabalya refugee camp in the Gaza Strip. Family members said that the boy's father, Waled Izz el Din, and grandfather, Abdel Rahman, were killed by gunfire, March 12, 2002.

Ahmed Jadallah

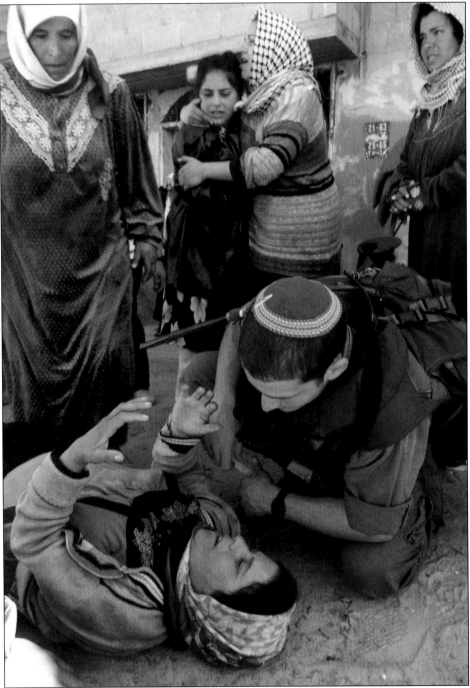

An Israeli medic assists a Palestinian woman who had fainted when Jewish settlers went on a rampage in a Palestinian farm area of Kfar Yam in the Gush Katif Jewish settlement bloc in the Gaza Strip, January 15, 2001.

Jim Hollander

Nine-year-old Shai Plum salutes the grave of his older brother Baruch at his funeral in Tel Aviv, November 19, 2000. Staff Sergeant Baruch Plum, 21, was gunned down by a Palestinian police officer at his Israeli army post in the Gaza Strip.

Havakuk Levison

**Jim Hollander, November 2000**

I hadn't originally planned to attend the funeral of Israeli reservist Avner Shalom and was on another assignment.

On November 12, 2000, word began reaching us that a Russian plane had been hijacked and was heading for an Israeli military base in the Negev Desert, four hours from Jerusalem. I arrived just after the plane was allowed to land and managed to photograph the freed passengers.

But it was just one hour further south to Eilat where the funeral was to take place, and I decided to go.

I arrived just as hundreds of mourners, including soldiers who served alongside the dead man in an infantry brigade, were entering the cemetery. Shalom, 27, had been killed by Palestinian gunmen the previous day in a drive-by shooting in the Gaza Strip. The light was fading fast. The dead soldier's comrades-in-arms, friends and family members broke down in grief, crying, screaming and clutching one another as the body was quickly lowered into the grave and covered with earth, as is Jewish custom.

I left the funeral just after taking this photograph and was transmitting the image via satellite telephone from my car as the mourners slowly left the cemetery in the dark after a stark outpouring of raw emotion.

That same day, another Israeli soldier was buried in another part of Israel, and in the Gaza Strip, two Palestinian police officers and a 16-year-old Palestinian boy, all killed the day before by Israeli troops in clashes, were buried as well. Reuters photographers covered at least one funeral every day during this month of the Israeli–Palestinian conflict.

Jim Hollander

The mother (second left) and family of Mohammad al-Madhoun mourn in their home in Gaza, November 12, 2000. Madhoun was one of two Palestinians killed in a shoot-out with Israeli soldiers near the Jewish settlement of Kfar Darom in the Gaza Strip.

Jerry Lampen

An Israeli teenager mourns while holding a Hebrew prayer book at a candle
memorial on Ben-Yehuda Street, a pedestrian shopping mall, in central west
Jerusalem, September 5, 1997, where three suicide bombers the day before killed five
Israelis and wounded more than 170.

Jim Hollander

# Living Under Fire

## Reuters correspondents

---

### An Israeli Family's Story

Megan Goldin

Twins Eran and Avi Mizrahi were in a boisterous mood, celebrating their sixteenth birthday at a cafe in central Jerusalem with school friends on a Saturday night in December 2001.

As the twins opened their gifts to a rowdy rendition of birthday songs by their friends, two Palestinian suicide bombers were making their way to the cafe district with instructions to find a crowd of people and blow themselves up.

It would be the Mizrahi twins' last evening as fun-loving teenagers.

By the end of the night, two of their friends were dead and Eran lay comatose in an intensive care ward with a screw from the shrapnel-packed bomb lodged in the front lobe of his brain.

Nir Elias

Eran (right) and Avi Mizrahi at their home in Jerusalem, May 22, 2002.

"At about midnight I got a call from Avi who said, 'Dad, I was injured in the terror attack and Eran was badly wounded but I can't find him,'" their father Rafi Mizrahi recalled several months later, his hand on the shoulder of his wheelchair-bound son.

Eran fled for safety after the first bomber blew himself up. He ran into the path of the second attacker, who detonated his explosives seconds later. In all, 10 people were killed and more than 100 wounded in the double-barreled attack.

"When they evacuated Eran, they thought he was dead. They put him with the dead bodies. He had no pulse, he was not breathing," Mizrahi said.

Resuscitated by an alert medic, Eran was taken to surgery in a Jerusalem hospital, where his father finally located him by ringing his cellular telephone continuously until a nurse answered.

"It took seconds but it felt like forever," Mizrahi said.

An outstanding student, Eran was a prankster who often played comic roles in school plays but took his piano studies seriously, practicing regularly for eight years. He wanted to become a doctor.

Sixteen years after Mizrahi carried his newly born twin sons bundled up in blankets out of Jerusalem's Hadassah hospital, he and his wife were back at the same hospital, feeding and washing Eran in a 24-hour vigil.

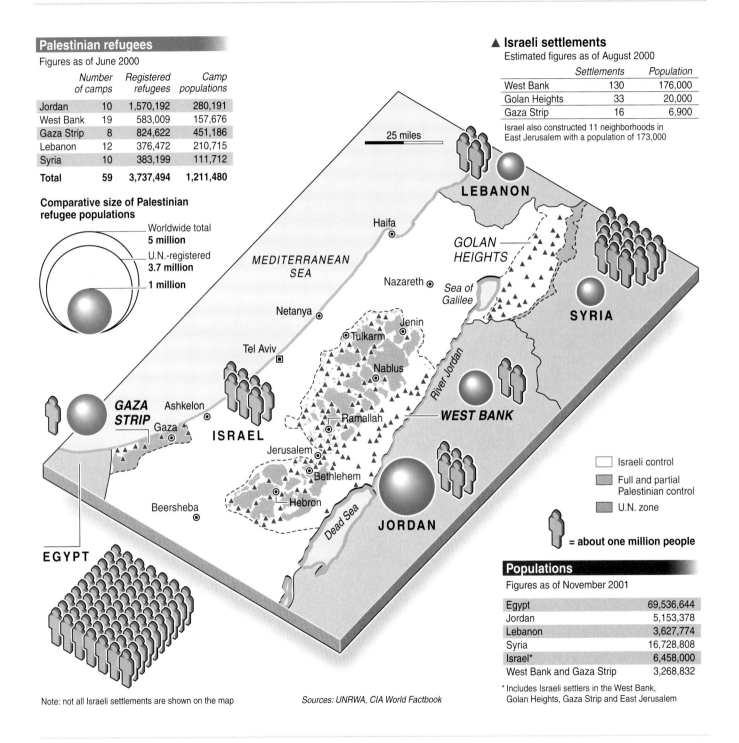

## Palestinian refugees

Figures as of June 2000

| | Number of camps | Registered refugees | Camp populations |
|---|---|---|---|
| Jordan | 10 | 1,570,192 | 280,191 |
| West Bank | 19 | 583,009 | 157,676 |
| Gaza Strip | 8 | 824,622 | 451,186 |
| Lebanon | 12 | 376,472 | 210,715 |
| Syria | 10 | 383,199 | 111,712 |
| **Total** | **59** | **3,737,494** | **1,211,480** |

**Comparative size of Palestinian refugee populations**

Worldwide total
**5 million**

U.N.-registered
**3.7 million**

**1 million**

## ▲ Israeli settlements

Estimated figures as of August 2000

| | Settlements | Population |
|---|---|---|
| West Bank | 130 | 176,000 |
| Golan Heights | 33 | 20,000 |
| Gaza Strip | 16 | 6,900 |

Israel also constructed 11 neighborhoods in East Jerusalem with a population of 173,000

25 miles

LEBANON

Haifa

GOLAN HEIGHTS

MEDITERRANEAN SEA

Nazareth

Sea of Galilee

SYRIA

Netanya

Jenin

Tulkarm

Tel Aviv

Nablus

River Jordan

GAZA STRIP

Ashkelon

Gaza

ISRAEL

Ramallah

WEST BANK

Jerusalem

Bethlehem

Beersheba

Hebron

Dead Sea

JORDAN

EGYPT

Israeli control

Full and partial Palestinian control

U.N. zone

= about one million people

## Populations

Figures as of November 2001

| | |
|---|---|
| Egypt | 69,536,644 |
| Jordan | 5,153,378 |
| Lebanon | 3,627,774 |
| Syria | 16,728,808 |
| Israel* | 6,458,000 |
| West Bank and Gaza Strip | 3,268,832 |

* Includes Israeli settlers in the West Bank, Golan Heights, Gaza Strip and East Jerusalem

Note: not all Israeli settlements are shown on the map

*Sources: UNRWA, CIA World Factbook*

"He can't speak but he can write a few words . . . two, three words and that's it," said Mizrahi, celebrating a minor victory after Eran scrawled "I love music" in English to an occupational therapist carrying out an assessment.

"The doctors are not saying anything. It's still too early, but it will take a lot of hope."

Eran's twin, Avi, suffered only minor physical injuries but Mizrahi said the emotional scars run deep.

"Avi saw white smoke when the terrorist blew himself up and he saw the bomber's body lying on the pavement before he was knocked to the ground by the second explosion."

Mizrahi does not blame Palestinians nor does he seek vengeance. His Arab friends have telephoned him to express sympathy, and an Arab neurosurgeon was among the doctors who performed four brain surgeries on Eran.

"I pity the Palestinian nation. They don't want this," said Mizrahi, who is bitter and angry over his son's fate.

"I blame Yasser Arafat. Who is Arafat? A man with blood on his hands who does not want peace with us. Israeli leaders are also to blame because they believed Arafat. They created him. Only the leaders are to blame for what happened to our children," he said.

## A Palestinian Family's Story

## Christine Hauser

When Muin Abu Lawyeh was shot in the neck and died on a mountain path, he was holding a school bag bought for his daughter Bahia, imprinted with words which resonated with tragic irony:

"Do not wage war," read the slogans on the bag. "Love everything that has life."

On a clear summer morning almost a year after the second Palestinian uprising broke out, Abu Lawyeh, a Palestinian carpenter, set out by foot from his village in the West Bank to the nearby city of Nablus to buy supplies for his daughter, who was due to attend school for the first time.

To reach the city from Salfit he had to hike over Mount Gezirim, scaling its rocky slopes and pushing through heavy brush to circumvent the Israeli checkpoints that carved Palestinian towns into cantons after the start of the uprising, or Intifada, against occupation in September 2000.

The journey cost him his life.

The Israeli army launched an investigation into the shooting of Abu Lawyeh by its troops, who are stationed in a post overlooking the trail from the city where it says Palestinians have smuggled explosives into the Jewish state.

When Abu Lawyeh died, the death toll in the Intifada was more than 500 Palestinians and over 100 Israelis, numbers that would more than double in the months to come.

Many of the faces of the dead faded quickly into obscurity, replaced by those of the next day's unrelenting violence.

But Abu Lawyeh's life exemplified that of many Palestinians living with the effects of Israeli occupation.

Before the uprising erupted, he worked for an Israeli businessman in the nearby Jewish settlement of Ariel, showing a permit to an armed guard at the gate every day to gain entrance.

His former boss said he was "a good man, a hard worker, an honest man."

But once the conflict started, Israel clamped down on Palestinian villages because of security concerns after suicide bombings killed scores of Israelis.

Muin Abu Lawyeh was shot in the neck and died on a mountain path.

Abed Omar Qusini

For Abu Lawyeh, the proximity of his village to the Jewish settlement went from an economic windfall to his downfall after he lost his job.

He tried to make ends meet by working in a shop outside the village, skirting West Bank checkpoints like thousands of other Palestinians to reach work or buy supplies in neighboring cities, such as on that fine morning in August.

The army initially said after Abu Lawyeh's death that its soldiers adhered to "regulations for detaining a suspect, in which they fired."

But the shooting of the 38-year-old carpenter, who was unarmed, raised questions which persisted nearly one year after his death.

Israeli media reported that the soldiers seriously violated rules of engagement. The Israeli human rights group B'Tselem said that Abu Lawyeh's case was an example of Israeli soldiers not following regulations.

"The Israeli army military police asked us for help in investigating the case," said Lior Yavne, a B'Tselem spokesman.

B'Tselem sent field workers to the spot where Abu Lawyeh was killed. Palestinians stream along the dirt path in beautiful rolling hills, on foot or on donkeys, for the nearly one-mile trek between their villages and the city. Tear gas canisters litter the ground.

After Abu Lawyeh's death, his widow Naja closed their house in Salfit and went to Nablus with her three children to stay with his mother.

She sat in the second-floor apartment as women from the city came to pay condolences, which she received with composure and dignity, her hands folded in her lap. Her hair was covered with a modest Muslim headscarf.

After the visitors left, Naja sat with me. She did not speak much, preferring to listen to her brother-in-law tell the tale of the life and death of the man she had married six years before.

She nodded vigorously when asked if Abu Lawyeh's former employer, the Jewish settler, treated them well.

When family members went to another room to fetch the plastic bag of school supplies Abu Lawyeh had been carrying when he was shot, she slumped slightly in her seat.

And when they took out the clothes he had been wearing, she silently buried her face in her hands, unable to look at the trousers still dusty on one side from the morning when he fell dead, shot on a remote mountain path.

## A Soldier's Story

# Jeffrey Heller

Tal Feist, 28, is a member of Israel's own baby-boomer generation, born after tens of thousands of reservists came home from the Sinai desert and Golan Heights battlefronts of the 1973 Middle East war.

He has known little peace since his conscription at the age of 18. Feist spent part of his three years in the regular army in southern Lebanon, where soldiers in an Israeli-declared "security zone" came under frequent attack by Hizbollah guerrillas.

Havakuk Levison

Tal Feist, reservist lieutenant and architecture student at his desk in Tel Aviv.

Now an architecture student in Tel Aviv, the reservist lieutenant is called into uniform for about a month each year and is likely to remain a citizen-soldier at least until the age of 40.

Feist has done two reserve stints in the West Bank, in the cities of Bethlehem and Hebron, since the Palestinian uprising against occupation erupted in September 2000.

"They tear you away from civilian life and suddenly you have to be a reservist for 30 days. It is very hard," said Feist, who got married last year.

"After you complete your stint, you know you won't get another call-up notice in the mail for at least another two months. But after that, every few days, you know you are going to see it and the boom drops. It's not a good feeling."

Like many Israelis who thought interim accords with the Palestinians heralded peace, Feist, who said he held left-wing views, has had to face the hard reality of a Palestinian revolt and suicide attacks in Israeli cities.

"There was hope of peace and it blew up in our face," he said. "Suddenly you have to defend your country and give it all you've got so that it won't collapse."'

Things seemed simpler back in Lebanon.

"When I was an 18-year-old soldier and then a 21-year-old soldier, they would say we had to stand up to Hizbollah and protect the northern border. You faced a guerrilla organization and you knew it was your enemy," Feist said.

But, he said, the West Bank presented a dilemma for reservists like himself who can identify with ordinary Palestinians under Israeli guns.

"Now you are in a confrontation with a civilian population. It raises many questions. We spoke about this on patrol. We know how they feel.

"If I see a Palestinian and stop him to check his ID, it's not pleasant, but I try to do it with a bit more respect and sensitivity. I'll ask him how he is doing and wish him well."

For many Palestinians aspiring to a state of their own, it is the uniform of the occupying power, not the man behind it, that they see.

"Some of those you stop are very frightened and they do things automatically. There are those who worked in Israel

and know we are only doing our job. Then there are the ones who are hostile because of the situation and you feel the hate—I know they don't like me, but I forgive them," Feist said.

## A Palestinian Police Officer's Story

### Nidal al-Mughrabi

Ahmed Eid long dreamt of becoming a schoolteacher, but in the end the lure of a job with a uniform proved more inviting.

Eid became a lieutenant in the Palestinian police force, a job that earned him only $300 a month but made him feel part of Palestinian efforts to build a civil society after the 1993 Oslo peace accords.

As a police officer in the Gaza Strip, he also played a role in the Palestinian uprising against Israeli occupation.

"When I put on the police uniform for the first time, I felt happy and secure. I felt I had made up for years of fear and insecurity," said Eid, 27.

Palestinians saw the establishment of their first security agencies as a symbol of independence from Israel's occupation.

Eid, assigned to the criminal investigation department, felt he was taking part in building a civil society after years in which militia groups had meted out punishment to suspects under a system of "rough justice."

"I represent the law. It was a great thing to build an army and prepare for a state," he said.

Eid shared the dream of millions of Palestinians in the Gaza Strip, the West Bank and the diaspora, and found himself increasingly ready to defend that dream.

"At the start we saw children's lives being wasted by merciless Israeli soldiers as we looked on," Eid said. "Soon we had to get involved, regardless of orders of restraint by our superiors."

Young Palestinian stone throwers were a large proportion of those killed in the early stages of the uprising in battles with Israeli forces, despite what the Israeli army called a policy of restraint.

Later the Palestinians turned increasingly to guerrilla-style warfare and suicide bombings, while Israeli forces staged more raids into Palestinian-ruled areas. Clashes erupted frequently between Israeli soldiers and armed Palestinians, including police officers.

Dozens of Eid's fellow police officers were killed, some in gunbattles with Israeli soldiers, others during Israeli army incursions and others carrying out attacks against Israelis.

Eid said life as a police officer was far from easy. Israel bombed, shelled or flattened most of the Palestinian security headquarters, detained dozens of policemen and undermined the security forces' ability to operate.

When he first joined the police force, Eid did not expect to fight helicopter gunships and tanks. The conflict has affected his private life as well, persuading him to delay plans to get married until the conflict dies down.

"There is no joy these days. Nothing is stable," Eid said.

"If I survive this fighting in one piece I'll get married and start a family."

Palestinian police forces exceed 40,000 in self-rule areas, providing security for the more than three million residents of Gaza and the West Bank.

"We were told we would spread the philosophy of peace," he said. "But Israel imposed on us all the logic of war."

Eid had hoped for a better future.

"Things cannot go on like this. There must be a solution," he said. "We and the Israelis need peace and we both have to acknowledge each other's needs."

## A Palestinian Militant's Story

## Matt Spetalnick

"Abu Ali" sipped sweet tea as he sat at a bare table in a dimly lit hideout adorned with posters of Hamas gunmen and suicide bombers. Then, staring straight ahead at the yellowing wallpaper, he described in a slow, measured voice what went through his mind each time he took aim down the barrel of his M-16 assault rifle.

"You keep in your head that every Israeli is part of an occupying army in our holy Palestine," the tall, 28-year-old Palestinian said during a secretly arranged meeting inside a cinderblock building in the West Bank town of Jenin. "It is our legitimate right to kill them."

THE ISRAELI-PALESTINIAN CONFLICT    crisis in the middle east

Abu Ali (his *nom de guerre*) said he spent six years in Israeli prisons because of his membership in the military wing of Hamas, a Muslim fundamentalist group sworn to the destruction of Israel.

By the time he was released in mid-2001, the Palestinian uprising against Israeli occupation—the second Intifada—was already raging across the West Bank and Gaza Strip.

Instead of taking time to savor his freedom, Abu Ali purchased a smuggled M-16 from an Israeli arms dealer and rejoined the ranks of Hamas fighters in the Jenin refugee camp in the northern West Bank.

The Jenin he returned to had become a hotbed of militancy. Hamas had buried its differences with rival factions there, joining forces to carry out suicide attacks and raid Jewish settlements.

Like many of his Muslim brethren, Abu Ali accepted the words of the Hamas clerics who preached that a martyr—one who died in the act of "jihad," or holy war—would be rewarded with an instant ticket to paradise.

That proved such a tempting offer to young men in Jenin that Hamas had to turn away volunteers for suicide missions, Abu Ali said.

During the months that followed, Jenin's refugee quarters became the launching pad for some of the bloodiest suicide attacks Israelis had ever endured, and the Israeli army branded the camp a "breeding ground for terror."

At one point, Abu Ali toyed with the idea of undertaking a "martyr bombing" himself. But he ultimately decided he could do more fighting for the Palestinian nationalist cause than dying for it.

He didn't have to wait long for the battle to begin.

On April 3, 2002, after a Hamas bomber blew himself up, killing 29 people during a Passover celebration at an Israeli hotel, tanks and armored bulldozers smashed their way into Jenin.

Abu Ali and his fellow fighters hunkered down in the narrow alleys, spraying gunfire and setting booby-traps, but they were outnumbered and outgunned. He said dozens of his comrades were killed along with 23 Israeli soldiers. He survived by hiding out for days beneath the rubble.

Resurfacing after the Israeli pullout, Abu Ali looked drawn and haggard. His new khaki outfit hung loosely on his lean frame. Still, he vowed to help Hamas regroup its cells in Jenin and fight on.

But it was clear he was living like a wanted man, rarely venturing out by day, sleeping in a different place every night. He had no home to go back to, since it was flattened during the Israeli invasion.

Though he had married and fathered a child shortly after his release from prison, he was rarely able to see his new family.

It was not the life he had dreamed of as a boy. The son of a common laborer who fled Haifa during the first Arab-Israeli war in 1948, Abu Ali earned good grades and wanted to study medicine.

Instead, after finishing high school, he was drawn to Hamas and its potent mix of Islamic radicalism and Palestinian nationalism. "I am Hamas because it is pure and offers no concessions to the Israelis," he said.

Abu Ali insists he is anything but a natural-born killer. But he said as long as Israeli troops occupied Arab land and killed Palestinians, Hamas fighters would have no qualms about drawing Israeli blood and targeting civilians.

"It is our revenge, a natural reaction," he said, "As it is written in the Jews' own Bible—an eye for an eye."

## An Architect's Tale

# Michele Gershberg

Amid the bloodshed and sorrow of the past two years, the death of Avi Boaz stands out as particularly tragic.

Boaz, 71, was an architect, a man who tried to build bridges across the warring communities. A Jew and a Zionist, who came from the United States, Boaz lived in the Israeli settlement of Maale Adumim outside Jerusalem. But much of his time was spent in the nearby West Bank town of Beit Jala, where he worked and found companionship with his many Palestinian friends.

His daughter, Idit Cohen, said Boaz first ventured into Beit Jala shortly after the 1967 Middle East war when he was asked to help restore the old Arab stone buildings in the area.

"That's when his romance with the Arabs began, and it continued to the last day of his life," she said. "He knew Arabic better than Hebrew. He would eat with them, he would even travel with them abroad and he was like a very good friend, a brother, one of the family."

Cohen repeatedly warned her father against the dangers of traveling in the West Bank, particularly after the outbreak of the Palestinian uprising.

"He would always say—I am Avi Boaz, everyone knows me and nothing will happen to me," she recalled.

On January 15, 2002, Boaz went to have lunch with his friend of 34 years, Jamal al-Arja, in Beit Jala. On his way back, four Palestinian gunmen snatched him at a checkpoint, drove his vehicle to a soccer field in nearby Beit Sahour, got out of the car and fired at him 20 times through the windshield.

al-Arja was angry and heartbroken at the death of his friend. "How would you feel if someone in your family was killed? He was one of the family...his daughter was born here," he said. "He loved life with the Arabs. Even when there was shooting in Beit Jala, he was here."

Boaz's daughter told of a man who was always optimistic and whose faith in his friends never waned despite a daily tempest of bloodshed and destruction.

"If he had only been wounded and came out alright, he would still be going there [Beit Jala] today. Because he always believed things would be good in the end," she said.

Boaz moved from the United States to Israel in 1961, but never took Israeli citizenship even though his wife, Eve, and daughter did. A childhood disability left him nearly lame, and until his death he walked with the help of a cane.

He opened an architectural practice with a Palestinian partner in Beit Jala, shopped in the markets and ate at the

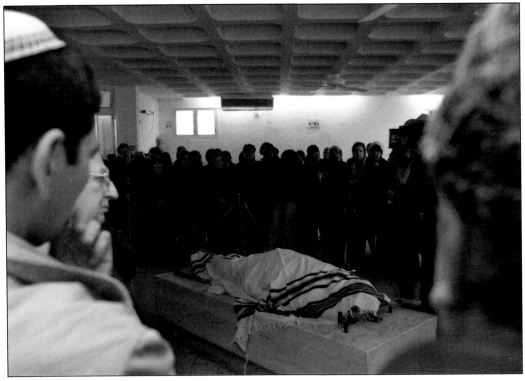

Nir Elias

Relatives and friends of Avi Boaz attend his funeral in Jerusalem, January 16, 2002.

al-Arjas' hotel almost every day. Boaz and al-Arja celebrated the births of each other's children and traveled to Jordan and Egypt together. For the wedding of one of Arja's sons, Boaz decorated his Rover convertible with flowers to pick up the bride. That was the same car in which he met his death.

On the fateful day, Boaz drove off after lunch with Bashir al-Arja, one of Jamal's sons. When they reached a nearby Palestinian police checkpoint, gunmen waiting nearby approached the car bearing Israeli license plates and ordered Bashir to leave. When he refused, hoping to protect his friend, the gunmen drove away with the two in Boaz's car.

Along the way to Beit Sahour, they dumped a beaten Bashir out of the car. Boaz's bullet-riddled body was found later that evening.

At his funeral, family and friends spoke of one of Boaz's last acts in life. Long divorced, Boaz remarried his wife, Eve, as she lay dying of cancer in a Jerusalem hospital in late 2001, hoping to bind their family together again.

Ten days after her death, Boaz was buried next to his wife.

Jerry Lampen

Palestinian medical students watch an Israeli tank and soldiers as they try to
cross a checkpoint near the Jewish settlement of Kfar Darom near Khan Younis
in the southern Gaza Strip, November 23, 2000.

Jim Hollander

Barefoot Palestinian girls remove garbage in the Jabalya refugee camp in the Gaza Strip, May 14, 1987.

Ahmed Jadallah

Palestinians sit on a Gaza Strip beach smoking water pipes and enjoying the sunshine, February 27, 2002.

Jim Hollander

A Jewish settler prays at the window of a mobile home set up in a bid to expand the
Beit El settlement situated outside the West Bank city of Ramallah. He is wearing
*tefillin*, which consist of small boxes containing prayer parchments.

Jim Hollander

An armed Israeli settler runs for cover outside the Palestinian city of Nablus as a gunbattle erupts between Palestinians, Jewish settlers and Israeli soldiers, October 12, 2000.

Damir Sagolj

Palestinians are reflected in a broken mirror as they walk in a refugee camp in Rafah
in the southern Gaza Strip, April 15, 2001, a day after Israeli forces attacked the camp.

**Desmond Boylan, May 2001**

I took this picture in the Brazil Refugee Camp in Rafah, which is in the southern Gaza Strip bordering Egypt. It is one of the most dangerous and deprived places in the occupied territories. There are constant gunbattles between Israeli forces and Palestinian gunmen, and journalists' movements are very limited, because of the danger.

On the night before the picture was taken and early that morning, Israeli bulldozers backed by tanks entered the camp and demolished about two dozen houses. When I arrived in the camp, residents were wandering around. I saw some women and children climbing over the rubble, and the girl in the picture was among them. I remember feeling very uneasy. I sat for a while in the rubble, not really taking any pictures but worrying about the sporadic machine-gun fire that rang out every few minutes.

Whenever there were shots, people ran for cover and there was confusion and shouting. I stayed down low in the rubble, watching a family looking for their belongings.

Suddenly I saw the mirror with the reflection of the girl and shot the picture. She seemed to be in a daze, ignoring the shooting, just sitting there. I felt like speaking to her but didn't. The sight of her sitting like that filled me with sadness.

Desmond Boylan

Yannis Behrakis

Hassan, a 19-year-old Palestinian refugee, is greeted by his nephews in the Dheisheh refugee camp on the outskirts of Bethlehem, January 4, 2001. The Dheisheh refugee camp has been home to thousands of Palestinian refugees since 1948.

Ali Jarekji

Ahmed (right) and Bilal look out of their kitchen window from their metal shanty
house in the Palestinian refugee camp of Baqaa near Amman, Jordan, January 2, 2001.

A Palestinian woman sits in the destroyed kitchen of her home in the Gaza Strip town of Khan Younis, July 13, 2001.

Reinhard Krause

Jim Hollander

Palestinian boys peer through the windows of a mosque in Gaza City as they stand on the roof trying to see the funeral of Yahya Ayyash, known as "The Engineer," taking place inside, January 6, 1996.

Palestinian women, seen through bullet holes, walk in the Rafah refugee camp in the southern Gaza Strip, November 27, 2001.

Reinhard Krause

# Leaders in War and Peace

## Reuters correspondents

### Yasser Arafat

Wafa Amr

The grainy pictures of Yasser Arafat by candlelight, a prisoner in his own office in Ramallah, went round the world.

In his long-range stand-off with Israeli nemesis Ariel Sharon, Arafat worked the cell phone and international media to mobilize world public opinion.

But when the Palestinian leader emerged from the month-long siege by Israeli troops, it was by no means clear whether his position was stronger or weaker.

He was hated and mistrusted by most Israelis, even those who once favored signing a peace treaty with him; he had lost the confidence of the United States; and pressure to reform his Palestinian Authority was growing.

The uncertainty surrounding Arafat seemed typical. For in an extraordinary career, he has known both triumph and disaster.

Reuters Television

Palestinian President Yasser Arafat, in a candle-lit interview at his ruined West Bank headquarters in Ramallah, asks the world to end what he called Israel's assault on his people, March 30, 2002.

In 1974 he strode to the United Nations podium, a weapon demonstrably strapped to his waist, saying he bore an olive branch and freedom fighter's gun. "Do not let the olive branch fall from my hands," he told the General Assembly.

But by 1982 Arafat and his fighters had been expelled by the Israelis from Beirut, and he was forced into exile in Tunis. Eleven years later he was shaking hands with Israeli Prime Minister Yitzak Rabin at the White House and winning the Nobel Peace Prize. Eight years after that came the siege of his office in Ramallah.

Arafat has always said that he has toiled, first as a guerrilla leader and then as a statesman, to put Palestine on the map of the Middle East. He says he has turned over every stone to seek an end to Israel's occupation and establish statehood.

Has he squandered his chances?

Israel says he rejected an offer by then Prime Minister Ehud Barak of up to 95 percent of the occupied territories at the Camp David summit with U.S. President Bill Clinton in the summer of 2000.

Arafat counters that Barak never put the offer on the table and that he could never have accepted ideas that would maintain Israeli occupation of most of East Jerusalem and other parts of the West Bank. An aide to Clinton, Robert Malley, also has said the Palestinians were not offered a settlement they could accept.

One thing is clear. The talks broke up in bitterness. Within months, the second Palestinian Intifada had begun. And as Palestinians rallied to the cause, Arafat was once again the personification of their nationhood.

"Arafat emerged as a leader, a hero and a symbol of resistance. This culture of resistance will not die away," said Palestinian political analyst Mahdi Abdul Hadi.

During the siege of Ramallah, the 72-year-old leader slept on the floor, making sure all others with him were covered up. People with him said he never complained about shortages of water when taking medicine.

For Israelis it underlined the impression that in some ways Arafat was more comfortable in his role as guerrilla leader defying the enemy than as diplomat. For his people it reflected defiance and rejection of Israeli dictates.

## Key players in the region

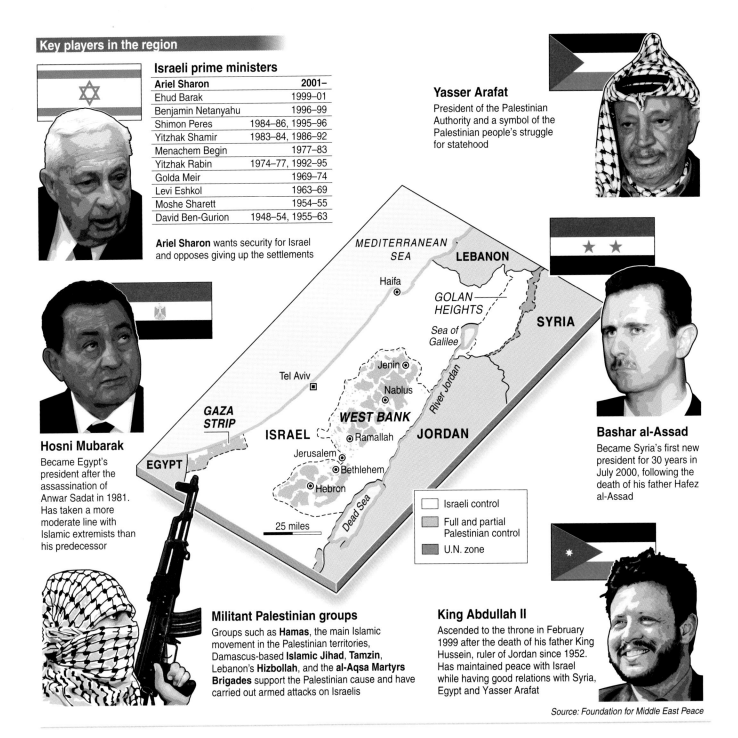

### Israeli prime ministers

| Ariel Sharon | 2001– |
|---|---|
| Ehud Barak | 1999–01 |
| Benjamin Netanyahu | 1996–99 |
| Shimon Peres | 1984–86, 1995–96 |
| Yitzhak Shamir | 1983–84, 1986–92 |
| Menachem Begin | 1977–83 |
| Yitzhak Rabin | 1974–77, 1992–95 |
| Golda Meir | 1969–74 |
| Levi Eshkol | 1963–69 |
| Moshe Sharett | 1954–55 |
| David Ben-Gurion | 1948–54, 1955–63 |

**Ariel Sharon** wants security for Israel and opposes giving up the settlements

### Yasser Arafat

President of the Palestinian Authority and a symbol of the Palestinian people's struggle for statehood

### Bashar al-Assad

Became Syria's first new president for 30 years in July 2000, following the death of his father Hafez al-Assad

### Hosni Mubarak

Became Egypt's president after the assassination of Anwar Sadat in 1981. Has taken a more moderate line with Islamic extremists than his predecessor

MEDITERRANEAN SEA

LEBANON

Haifa

GOLAN HEIGHTS

Sea of Galilee

SYRIA

Jenin

Tel Aviv

Nablus

River Jordan

GAZA STRIP

WEST BANK

ISRAEL

Ramallah

JORDAN

Jerusalem

Bethlehem

EGYPT

Hebron

Dead Sea

25 miles

- Israeli control
- Full and partial Palestinian control
- U.N. zone

### Militant Palestinian groups

Groups such as **Hamas**, the main Islamic movement in the Palestinian territories, Damascus-based **Islamic Jihad**, **Tamzin**, Lebanon's **Hizbollah**, and the **al-Aqsa Martyrs Brigades** support the Palestinian cause and have carried out armed attacks on Israelis

### King Abdullah II

Ascended to the throne in February 1999 after the death of his father King Hussein, ruler of Jordan since 1952. Has maintained peace with Israel while having good relations with Syria, Egypt and Yasser Arafat

*Source: Foundation for Middle East Peace*

Ahmed Jadallah

Palestinian police officers hang a picture of President Yasser Arafat from their destroyed police building in the Gaza Strip, November 21, 2000.

Arafat has never been a man to show any enjoyment of personal comforts. He does not deal with money personally. His aides say he does not even know how much his shoes and clothes cost, because they are bought for him. He refuses to buy expensive things and once punished a bodyguard for buying him a pair of boots for a little under $100. From that day on, the bodyguard bought Arafat clothes and footwear without telling him how much they cost.

He loves to watch cartoons, which help him relax, and his favorite is *Tom and Jerry*. In Casablanca in 1994 he became angry when a Saudi official refused to see him and had talks with PLO official Faisal al-Husseini instead. As the meeting dragged on, Arafat paced up and down the room, shouted at his aides and then settled down to watch cartoons on television. He gradually started to unwind, and it was only after the cartoons finished that his aides dared talk to him again.

Ahmed Jadallah

Palestinian President Yasser Arafat helps to carry the coffin at the funeral of Hisham Mikki, 54, the head of the Palestinian Broadcasting Corporation, who was shot dead in Gaza Strip, January 18, 2001. The al-Aqsa Martyrs Brigades said its "anticorruption" unit killed him.

Israeli Prime Minister Sharon has made no secret of the fact that he regrets not having had him killed when he had the chance in Beirut in 1982. But the Israeli leader has always calculated that turning Arafat into a martyr would rebound against Israel.

Over the years, Arafat has become increasingly concerned with his legacy.

Palestinian poet Mahmoud Darwish has said Arafat does not want to be a legend. He simply wants to go down in history as the one to establish a Palestinian state. But the question remains: what kind of state and on what land?

"He will never accept a state made up of cantons, and Israelis don't want a just peace with the Palestinians, so Arafat's presence obstructs Israelis' dreams," Darwish said. "We have to believe Arafat when he says he would rather die a martyr than surrender."

Some aspects of Arafat's life remain shrouded in mystery.

Known to Palestinians as Abu Ammar or the Old Man, his real name is Mohammed Abdel-Raouf Arafat As Qudwa al-Hussaeini. He was born on August 24, 1929, in Cairo. His mother belonged to one of Jerusalem's leading families but died when Yasser, as he was called, was five years old. He was sent to live with his maternal uncle in Jerusalem, then under British rule, but returned to Egypt four years later. Arafat has revealed little about his childhood, but one of his earliest memories was of British soldiers breaking into his uncle's house after midnight, beating members of the family and smashing furniture.

Arafat fought in the 1948 war and was devastated by the Arab defeat. He earned a degree in engineering and in 1958 founded Al Fatah with a group of friends. At the end of 1964, Arafat left a contracting business he had established in Kuwait to become a full-time revolutionary, organizing Fatah raids into Israel from Jordan.

He took over the chairmanship of the Palestine Liberation Organization, an umbrella group of several different factions. Until 1970, the organization operated in Jordan, but it was expelled by King Hussein in what became known as "Black September." Arafat moved his forces to Lebanon, where they quickly became a dominant force in the south of the country, carrying out operations against Israeli towns and cities and civilian and military targets. It was not until 1974 that Arab governments recognized the PLO as the "sole legitimate representative of the Palestinian people," and the United Nations followed suit later that year.

When Arafat was driven out of Beirut in 1982, he set up his headquarters in Tunis. His international legitimacy grew during the first Intifada, which began in 1987.

Arafat parted company with many of his colleagues when he signed the 1993 peace deal which allowed him finally to return to historical Palestine and establish offices in Ramallah and Gaza.

In the relatively calm years during which he ran the Palestinian Authority in the 1990s, before the outbreak of the second Intifada in 2000, Arafat was accused of allowing corruption to flourish in the territories and failing to build democratic institutions or an independent judiciary. Palestinian children continued to learn from school books that demonized Israel and denied its legitimacy.

Now again, Arafat stands at a crossroads. The choice remains the same, with the olive branch in one hand and the pistol at his side.

Ariel Sharon with his head wrapped in a bandage after he was injured in the Sinai during the 1973 Yom Kippur War.

## Ariel Sharon

## Jeffrey Heller

One photograph of Ariel Sharon is seared into Israel's collective memory.

The black-and-white picture shows a rugged general, his head bandaged from a wound, in the Sinai desert where he led Israeli tanks across the Suez Canal into Egypt to turn the tide of the 1973 Middle East war.

With Israel's mighty army once more at his command, Prime Minister Sharon has met a Palestinian uprising against Israeli occupation with an iron fist aimed at his old nemesis, Yasser Arafat, a man he accused of being a terrorist and murderer.

Jim Hollander

**Jim Hollander, February 2001**

In February 2001, Ariel Sharon followed in the footsteps of his predecessors the morning after being elected Israel's prime minister. He touched the stones of the Western Wall and prayed at this holy site.

I had been there before. I had photographed many other leaders casting their eyes skyward as they stood before this monumental stone symbol of Jewish heritage.

Watching Sharon, the thought went through my mind that surely those who pray at this holy place recite the same silent prayers to similar universal ideals such as an end to poverty, hunger, disease and conflict.

On the one hand, it was just another "photo-op," and as photojournalists we were there to record the event for posterity.

But as I photographed Sharon in the midst of the second Intifada, I couldn't stifle my private hopes that maybe this time there would be change, maybe things would get better and maybe there would be peace.

Both Arafat, 72, and Sharon, 74, rose to the conflict.

Sharon breezed past the weekly stakeout of television cameras outside the Israeli cabinet room with his trademark lumbering gait and there's-work-to-do gaze—a flashback to his 25 years in the military, as if he were back in the war room charting plans against Israel's enemies.

A defiant Arafat still stood as a thorn in Sharon's side, declaring in cascading tones his willingness to die for the cause and his hopes to be a martyr for an independent Palestine. He denied any links with the attacks on Israelis.

To many Arabs, Sharon was reviled as the "butcher of Beirut," their reference to the killing of hundreds of Palestinians by Lebanese Christian militiamen in two refugee camps surrounded by Israeli troops in September 1982.

Israelis, who demonstrated in tens of thousands against Sharon after the massacres at the Sabra and Shatila camps in 1982, rallied behind his tough approach to the Palestinians, seeing him as a leader who could restore a sense of security.

It took Sharon almost two decades to rebuild his career after an Israeli inquiry found him "indirectly responsible." Sharon had to quit the defense ministry in disgrace, and it seemed he would never achieve his ambition of becoming prime minister. But he won the job by a landslide on February 6, 2001, on a promise to restore security for Israelis shellshocked by war after so much talk of peace with the Palestinians.

Few voters were fooled by pastoral campaign commercials shot on Sharon's farm that showed a grandfatherly figure tending his sheep, suggesting the Likud party lion was also capable of lying down with the lamb.

Nir Elias

Israeli Prime Minister Ariel Sharon (right) and Foreign Minister Shimon Peres attend a ceremony on the border with Jordan near the Israeli port city of Eilat, February 28, 2002.

As his long-time friend, right-wing Israeli journalist Uri Dan, put it at the time: "There is no new Sharon."

Reporters who regularly accompanied Sharon on foreign visits could attest to his courteous demeanor—and that the double-edged side of the old soldier had not faded away.

"Feel free to print whatever you want," he said at the start of one trip. "You won't be banned from the plane."

But, careful not to lose his temper, he nonetheless flashed withering glares at reporters who asked questions he did not like.

It was the "old Sharon" who fueled Arab anger by paying a heavily guarded visit on September 28, 2000, to the Temple Mount, setting the scene for the outbreak of a second Palestinian uprising.

Sharon faced the Palestinian uprising and suicide attacks by gradually ratcheting up Israeli military action while backing away from the brink of all-out war under pressure from the United States.

Under Sharon's command, the military used warplanes, attack helicopters, naval gunboats, armor and infantry to smash Palestinian Authority buildings and security headquarters.

Bounding off a helicopter to visit troops in the field, an ebullient Sharon appeared to be in his element, a battle-hardened veteran of all of Israel's wars.

As head of a special commando unit in the 1950s, Sharon dealt harshly with Arab infiltration into Israel from the West Bank and Gaza Strip and ruthlessly suppressed Palestinian guerrilla activity in Gaza in the 1970s.

Long regarded as a loose cannon by his superiors, Sharon left the army in June 1973 to pursue a political career and helped to found Likud, the party he now leads.

He was recalled to active duty in October 1973 after Egypt and Syria launched attacks against Israeli occupation forces in the Sinai and Golan Heights. Sharon emerged a war hero, having led tank forces made up of reservists across the Suez Canal into Egypt.

Yet Sharon said he would like to be remembered as a man of peace.

"For a long time, people would describe me as a general looking for wars," he once said.

"I was seriously wounded twice and felt all the excruciating pain in hospital. I had to make life-and-death decisions about others and about myself. Therefore, I can be so bold to say that I understand the importance of peace much better than many politicians who talk about peace but never withstood the tests I did or experience what I experienced.

"But peace has to be a real peace . . . and peace has to give the Jewish people security. We have to remember the Jews have one tiny country . . . the only place where Jews have the right and privilege to defend themselves, by themselves."

## Anwar Sadat

## David Rogers

He hadn't looked so cheerful for months. After a long, difficult summer, when anti-government rioters had returned to the streets of Cairo, the 1981 Army Day parade offered Anwar Sadat military spectacle, a television audience and another chance to relive battlefield glories.

He was 62, 11 years in power, a globally recognized statesman who had gambled spectacularly to force change in the Middle East and hold onto the presidency of a country beset with seemingly insurmountable economic and social woes.

Now, one of those gambles was about to cost him his life.

Immaculately uniformed as ever, refreshed after a break at his Alexandria beach villa, he was surrounded by generals as he took the salute. He had the attention of the diplomatic corps, sitting a few rows behind the presidential box, and in the same grandstand, 20 yards to his left, the international media, where I was seated.

The noisy march past was nearing its climax when it happened. Suddenly we realized that bullets were being fired. Live bullets. And this was not part of the scripted show.

With a few off-target shots ricocheting into the stand high above me, I dived to the ground, landing on top of a fellow British journalist. As the firing died, we picked ourselves up. The grandstand was a tangle of toppled chairs and bodies; the unlucky ones were dead or wounded.

The fatal moment came as soldiers ran from a truck in the passing parade and raised their rifles over the dais, aiming bullet after bullet into Sadat's powder-blue tunic. His body was carried to a helicopter but he was dead by the time he reached the hospital.

Photos of his tunic, peddled illicitly around news bureaus a few days later, showed it had been shot to shreds.

His assassins, rapidly rounded up and put on trial, were Islamic militants extracting their revenge for Sadat's peace agreement with Israel.

Sadat had been high profile since he launched the 1973 Middle East war, sending his army across the Suez Canal to drive back some of the Israeli forces occupying the Sinai desert on the other side of the waterway. On the back of Egypt's early successes, Sadat proclaimed the whole war a "victory," overlooking his army's later defeats.

He declared Egypt had exorcised its humiliation in the 1956 and 1967 conflicts with Israel.

Whatever the outcome, it enabled him to take a firm grip on power after a shaky start in the presidency. Succeeding the charismatic pan-Arabist Gamal Abdel Nasser, Sadat, according to a U.S. envoy at the time, wouldn't last more than six weeks.

Israeli Government Press Office

Egyptian President Anwar Sadat speaks with Israeli Prime Minister Menachem Begin on his historic trip to Jerusalem in 1977.

It was a failed prediction which Sadat, a village boy from the Nile Delta, loved recalling.

Boldness and blunt verbosity were his trademarks. He was more media aware and more accessible than any Arab leader.

Even when he went into prayer retreat for the final days of Ramadan, the holy month of fasting, he wanted the press nearby. One year his aides flew me to a monastic hideaway in the Sinai hinterland to be on hand should Sadat decide to break his desert silence. And he did.

He softened the repressive Socialist rule of the Nasser years and promoted a greater degree of freedom in Egypt—while assuring his photo stayed on the front page of the Cairo press.

He expelled thousands of Soviet military experts from Egypt—they were given a week to leave—and ended Moscow's powerful influence. Sadat built ever-closer ties with the United States, who, early in his rule, he identified as the only real power broker in the region and a far more generous source of aid and arms than the Soviet Union.

He sometimes courted controversy. Typically, Sadat stood by the Shah of Iran, an old ally, when he was deposed and, despite the anger of many in the Islamic world, offered the Shah sanctuary in Cairo.

Most dramatically of all, Sadat changed the face of the Middle East in 1977, flying at short notice to Jerusalem and later making peace with the Jewish state—a breathtaking step that stunned and split the Arab world, even his own cabinet.

A quarter of a century later, when one reads the speech he made to the Israeli Knesset (parliament), two prophetic passages stand out—his dire, insistent warning of repeated conflict until the Palestinian problem was solved and an acceptance that he had put himself at great risk by traveling to Jerusalem.

How great a risk became apparent on that blood-spattered, sun-baked Cairo parade ground four years later.

## Menachem Begin

## Patrick Massey

The telephone rang in my Tel Aviv office on a June morning in 1981 and a voice said, "The prime minister wants to speak to you." A short pause and on came the unmistakable tones of Menachem Begin.

"Mr. Massey, I want to apologize. Last night I told you our bombs had penetrated 40 meters of concrete to hit the nuclear plant in Baghdad. I was wrong. I should have said four meters. Please tell your readers."

I was stunned. Begin had indeed told me at a British Embassy garden party on the evening after the raid that Israeli bombs had burrowed 40 meters deep to destroy Iraq's rapidly developing nuclear installation. I and other reporters queried the figure, but Begin stuck to it.

After putting down the telephone, I reflected that most prime ministers making an error would have blamed the reporter for misquotation instead of calling to apologize. The incident illustrated the abundant complexities of Begin's character.

To me he never looked much like the firebrand nationalist that he undoubtedly was or the erstwhile militant leader accused of terrorism that many claimed him to be. Genial, humorous and a true master of oratory, he seemed more like a well-intentioned professor, patiently drumming lessons into the heads of obtuse students.

Nevertheless, there was no hiding Begin's determination to create a greater Land of Israel, stretching from the Mediterranean to the banks of the River Jordan. Withdrawal from what most of the world regarded as Palestinian land on the West Bank played no part in Begin's thinking.

Handing back Egypt's Sinai Peninsula was another matter. Unlike some of his even more hawkish colleagues, Begin saw clearly that this huge stretch of desert captured in the 1967 Six-Day War had no great value for Israel, provided it remained empty of potentially hostile troops. It was an offer President Anwar Sadat could not refuse. In 1979, swallowing his unease about the plight of the Palestinians, Sadat signed the peace agreement that was to prove his death warrant.

A restless impulsiveness pervaded Begin's character. One morning in 1981 he rose from his sickbed and to general astonishment announced the extension of Israeli "law, jurisdiction and administration" to the Golan Heights, captured from Syria in 1967.

The 1981 raid on Baghdad was another example. It happened long before Saddam Hussein had achieved demon status in the eyes of the West. There was then no great international concern about Iraq's nuclear program. Out of the blue Begin suddenly decided it would be a good idea to send out his air force and flatten the plant. Years later, when the United States went to war to expel Iraqi troops from Kuwait, some American military planners privately expressed their relief they did not have to deal with a nuclear-armed Baghdad.

Born in what was to become Poland, trained as a lawyer, Begin was imprisoned in Siberian labor camps by Stalin's secret police before making his way to Palestine in 1942. He had little rapport with the establishment of leftist Israelis who ran Israel from 1948 to 1977. In the 1940s he headed Irgun Zvai Leumi, one of the Jewish underground movements which fought to drive the British out of Palestine. The Irgun's actions included the hanging of two captured British army sergeants in retaliation for the execution of Irgun fighters and the blowing up of British headquarters at Jerusalem's King David Hotel which killed 91 people in 1946. Begin later said three telephone calls had been placed warning of the bombing in advance.

Terrorist? The very word was coined around that time to describe the activities of Begin and others like him. Like the host of people to whom that label has since been applied, Begin rejected it and called himself a fighter for freedom.

Thirty years on, many of my colleagues and I thought we discerned an essential humanity beneath that steely will. Begin finally crumbled in horror when Israeli troops that he sent into Lebanon became bogged down and took heavy casualties. The death of his wife Aliza deepened his depression. Still, his resignation in 1983 came as a total shock. After that, Begin became a virtual recluse, living in seclusion, glimpsed in public only at memorials for his

wife or at the wedding of a grandchild. He died on March 9, 1992, a sorrowful man.

## Yitzhak Rabin

## Robert Mahoney

I knew he was dead long before the announcement. A security contact phoned as soon as his wife Leah was taken into the icy Tel Aviv hospital room to see the body.

Yitzhak Rabin had been shot.

The news did not sink in. The radio was still saying he was wounded. He was strong. Israel needed him to pull through just as he had in the 1967 war.

I walked from the side office where I had taken the telephone call into the turmoil of the Jerusalem news room and asked a colleague to prepare a news flash.

The television switched live to the door of Ichilov hospital, which was besieged by journalists and distraught Israelis.

Rabin's right-hand man Eitan Haber emerged with a piece of paper.

"It is with regret," he read in Hebrew. We hit the button and brought the world the news that heralded the end of a historic experiment in Middle East peacemaking.

Rabin, the gruff general who had conquered Arab armies, had been felled by two bullets in the back from a Jewish assassin.

He won an election in 1992, promising Israelis shaken by years of Palestinian revolt and Saddam Hussein's Scud missiles that he would be their "Mr. Security." But he had not looked to his own safety. He refused to wear a

Yaacov Saar/Israeli Government Press Office

King Hussein of Jordan lights the cigarette of Prime Minister Yitzhak Rabin in the King's Aqaba Palace as the two meet after the official peace treaty signing ceremony held along the border, October 26, 1994.

bulletproof vest among his own people. His bodyguards were on alert for an Islamic suicide bomber at the peace rally that November 4 evening in 1995 but did not imagine a threat from one of their own.

Radical Palestinians had been incensed by the peace accord Rabin sealed with a handshake on the White House lawn two years earlier with Yasser Arafat.

But as Rabin walked to his car, it was a religious Jew, Yigal Amir, who stepped from the backstage gloom and opened fire. Rabin died in the back of his armored Cadillac, the bloodstained lyrics of the peace song he had just sung with the crowd crumpled in his pocket.

Jews like Amir saw Rabin as a traitor who had sold to Palestinians their biblical birthright to settle the West Bank of the Jordan River.

Just days before his death some demonstrators depicted Rabin in a Nazi uniform. That hurt the son of Russian and Ukrainian immigrants who had fought to create the state of Israel in the 1940s.

Rabin had never been "soft" on the Arabs. As commander of the Harel Brigade in 1948 he oversaw the expulsion of 50,000 Arab civilians, including women and children, from the towns of Lydda (Lod) and Ramle near Tel Aviv.

Thirty-one years later he wrote in his memoirs about the expulsions with his matter-of-fact honesty, but a government political-censorship committee deemed this dark episode of Israeli history still too sensitive and ordered him to cut it.

As an army man and sabra (native-born Israeli), Rabin's first instinct was to be tough rather than diplomatic. When the Palestinians he had conquered as chief of staff in 1967 rose up 20 years later, he said Israel would break their bones. When Islamic militancy grew in 1992, he had more than 400 activists rounded up in Gaza and the West Bank and dumped over the border in Lebanon to world condemnation. Asked what made him think Lebanon would take the men, he replied frankly, "They had always done it before."

In interviews, cigarette in hand, Rabin did not duck questions about his weaknesses. He dismissed charges that he drank too much and admitted closeting himself for 24 hours of "deep emotional distress" 12 days before the outbreak of war in June 1967. Former President Ezer Weizman said he stood in for Rabin as army chief for two days during Rabin's collapse.

The episode was quickly overtaken by military success which saw Israeli forces capture the Old City of Jerusalem and the Golan Heights.

Rabin later entered politics and became Israel's first native-born prime minister from 1974 to 1977. His biggest achievement was ordering the Entebbe rescue mission of hijacked Israeli hostages in 1976. But he had indifferent success as prime minister, and his career seemed over after he was forced to resign over revelations that his wife had retained a foreign bank account, which was then illegal.

There followed 15 years in the political wilderness. A bitter Rabin retreated into a small, bare office in the Tel Aviv military headquarters of the Israeli general staff, where he waited, smoking incessantly, for another chance.

It came in 1992, when he beat career politician Shimon Peres for the leadership of the Labor party. Rabin's toughness and Peres' political skill proved a winning combination in elections later that year, and the pair embarked on the secret road that led to the Arafat handshake.

At the White House that day in September 1993, Rabin seemed nervous, but when his time came, he rose to the occasion, at one point uttering the heartfelt words, "Enough of blood and tears! Enough."

Rabin had gone from bonebreaker to peacemaker.

At his funeral two years later, Jordan's King Hussein said of Rabin: "I have never thought that the moment would come like this when I would grieve the loss of a brother, a colleague, and a friend, a man, a soldier, who met us on the opposite side of a divide. You lived as a soldier. You died as a soldier for peace."

## Shimon Peres

## Howard Goller

Shimon Peres smiled. I had just asked him what Yitzhak Rabin said when they shook hands with Yasser Arafat to seal a groundbreaking Israeli-PLO peace deal in 1993. We on the sun-bleached White House lawn could hardly believe our eyes when Rabin, then prime minister, and Arafat, the Palestinian leader, reached across decades of war and enmity to shake hands. When next Arafat extended his right hand to Peres, Israel's foreign minister, Rabin pointed at Peres and said something.

"Now it's your turn," Rabin told him. It was "as though we are going to commit something of a terrible nature," Peres told me with a smile.

Nearly as surprising as the accord itself was the fact the gray-haired Peres and Rabin, rivals for decades, had made peace with each other to make history with the PLO, long Israel's Public Enemy Number One. Two years and two months later, minutes before a Jewish gunman killed Rabin for their peace moves, the prime minister hugged Peres at a peace rally.

"You see," Rabin told reporters. "Things change not only in the world but also in the Middle East—also for us."

Israel's perpetual prophet of peace, Shimon Peres never abandoned the political battlefield, even if it meant enduring the scorn of countrymen who tagged him a dreamer. Years after the handshakes, his Oslo peace deal in tatters, Peres clung to power, aspiring, he said, to help forge a better life for his children and grandchildren. His oratory and diplomacy made him a welcome visitor throughout the world, but he seemed out of place in the rough-and-tumble world of politics where Israelis branded him a loser and a schemer.

Although twice prime minister, Peres never won a national election outright in five tries. He failed even in a run for the largely ceremonial job of Israel's president. Even in defeat, Peres said he was reassured knowing that millions of Palestinians no longer lived under Israeli rule—a situation he called irreversible.

Negotiating with Arafat, Peres said, he knew he had to show respect. "Occasionally I warned myself, 'Don't be too

Gil Cohen Magen

With the Israeli flag in the foreground, Foreign Minister Shimon Peres speaks at a news conference in Jerusalem, March 6, 2002.

successful. It may be counterproductive. Don't press him too much. Don't try to squeeze out too much. You must be generous enough to enable him to remain a partner.'"

Asked if Arafat had shown him the same respect, Peres told me: "I am not sure. I think for him I was a strange continent … I think deep in his heart he understood that I am not an enemy, that I mean well, but he too … was afraid that I am trying to humiliate him, that I am trying to overpower him, that I am trying to push him in a corner."

During more than half a century of service, Peres held every top cabinet job. He was building Israel's defenses before the country's creation, albeit from an office rather than a battlefield. Israel's founding father, David Ben-Gurion, groomed him for leadership.

Widely regarded as having turned Israel into a nuclear power by procuring the secret Dimona reactor from France, he also oversaw Israel's rescue of hijacked Israelis at Entebbe in Uganda.

"If I would have to describe my biography, I would say 'From Dimona, where the reactor is, to Oslo, where the peace is,'" he told me in a 1996 interview. "I felt that Israel must become strong enough so she will be able to make peace."

## King Hussein

### Alistair Lyon

Flaming tires, smashed windows and crowds of angry Jordanians. Such scenes were shocking in the apparently placid Middle Eastern backwater I had been covering for two years.

Yet, price riots licked through outlying towns and for a few days in 1988 threatened to engulf Amman in the worst violence since King Hussein's Bedouin troops drove out Palestinian guerrillas in 1970 to 1971.

This time, the insurgents were not from Jordan's restive Palestinian majority. They were the East Bank tribesmen on whose loyalty the fragile Hashemite dynasty had always relied.

The king stuck by the IMF-prescribed price increases but placated the public by sacrificing his prime minister and calling Jordan's first general election since 1967.

For me, the episode illustrated how tenuous was the king's grip on power and how flexible he had to be to maintain it.

Until cancer killed him in February 1999, he had maneuvered skillfully through decades of war and shifting

Majed Jaber

U.S. Secretary of State Colin Powell, standing under portraits of Jordan's King Abdullah (right) and the late King Hussein, faces a news conference at Amman international airport, April 11, 2002.

Jim Hollander

Palestinian President Yasser Arafat introduces Jordan's King Hussein (center) to Rabbi Moshe Hirsch of the Neturei Karta, a tiny, anti-Zionist, ultra-Orthodox Jewish group which does not support the Jewish state of Israel, at Arafat's Gaza Strip offices, January 12, 1997.

alliances before leading his country into a 1994 peace treaty with Israel.

Yet King Hussein did not always get it right.

In his own view, his greatest mistake was to embroil Jordan in the 1967 Middle East war with the Jewish state, losing the West Bank and East Jerusalem and gaining 200,000 Palestinian refugees.

And in 1990, with Saddam Hussein a hero to most Jordanians, he failed to distance himself from Iraq's invasion of Kuwait, provoking the wrath of the United States, Saudi Arabia and other Gulf states that had previously bankrolled Jordan.

Despite this fall from American favor, he often seemed more admired in Israel and the West than in the Arab world.

Where some Arab leaders came across as unsavory, the diminutive, deep-voiced monarch reassured Westerners

with his impeccable English, courtly manners and soldierly bearing, not to mention his passions for flying, fast cars and women.

Generous to his foes, he had a regal presence and a personal touch—he was even polite to journalists, calling us Sir or Madam, and shaking hands after news conferences.

Educated at Britain's elite Harrow school and Sandhurst military academy, King Hussein inherited an impoverished desert country created almost as an afterthought by the imperial powers after World War One.

In 1951 he saw his grandfather, King Abdullah, who had annexed the West Bank the previous year following Israel's creation in 1948, killed by a Palestinian assassin on Jerusalem's Temple Mount. It was a trauma the future king never forgot.

Proclaimed king as a teenager in 1952 after his father proved mentally unfit to reign, he survived assassination attempts to become the longest-serving ruler in the Middle East.

Hussein made peace with Israel in 1994 after four decades of secret contacts with its leaders. Abroad he was acclaimed for the treaty, which won at best grudging acceptance at home.

Few could doubt his own commitment to peace, poignantly displayed in October 1998 when, wasted by chemotherapy, he left his sickbed to appeal to Israelis and Arabs to think of "our children and our children's children."

## Hafez al-Assad

## Bernd Debusmann

Obdurate. Machiavellian. Uncompromising. Intolerant. Calculating. Courteous. Patient. Persistent. Austere. Cunning. Clever. Complex. Scheming. Subtle. Authoritarian. Brutal. Ferocious. Hard. Aloof. Brilliant.

Each of these adjectives has been used to describe Hafez al-Assad in various stages of an extraordinary 30 years as president of Syria, but none more often than *ruthless*, a quality that ensured his survival against determined enemies and turned Syria into a stable, if cowed, country—in sharp contrast to the turbulent years between independence from France in 1946 to the 1970 coup that brought the former MIG-17 fighter pilot to power.

Before Assad, Syria lived through 22 coups and attempted coups. Under Assad, Syria set new landmarks for suppression of dissidents. After a series of acts of civil disobedience, bombings and assassinations of government officials and army officers in the late 1970s, Assad ordered

Syrian President Bashar al-Assad stands in front of a portrait of his late father, President Hafez al-Assad.

tanks and artillery to the northern city of Hama in 1982 to quell an uprising by citizens calling for an Islamic government. After blasting the center of the city day after day with tank and artillery fire, troops moved in and performed house-to-house searches. Estimates of the death toll range up to 30,000. The city center was a field of rubble. And anti-government protests ceased.

Assad's stamina was legendary, from working 16-hour days to making negotiating partners squirm in discomfort during marathon sessions that did not allow for bathroom breaks. During Henry Kissinger's shuttle diplomacy for Middle East peace in the early 1970s, U.S. diplomats preparing for talks with Assad were warned not to partake too freely of the coffee, tea and lemonade constantly urged on them. Interrupting their host with a request for a break would have been a breach of protocol. "Bladder diplomacy," one former ambassador termed it.

Journalism, it is said, provides the first drafts of history. We don't always get them right, especially when we predict. My early drafts of Syrian history were written during Assad's first seven-year term, and they touched all the subjects the Syrian government considered taboo: minority rule by the Muslim Alawite sect, widespread anti-government violence by the outlawed Muslim brotherhood, nepotism, corruption, a stifling bureaucracy, the lavish lifestyle and conspicuous consumption of Assad's brother Rifaat. On the seventh anniversary of Assad's seizure of power, I wrote a story that questioned whether the president could overcome his mounting problems and serve out his second seven-year term. He ruled another 23 years and died not by an assassin's bullet but a heart attack. So much for predictions.

The story was one of a string of reports that displeased Assad's government. Soon afterward, a gunman wielding a silenced pistol shot me in the back and ended my own seven years in the Middle East. There is no proof, but in a country as dominated by one man as Syria under Hafez al-Assad, I always suspected that assassinations and attempted assassinations of journalists in Beirut required at least a nod from the very top.

When Assad died, on June 10, 2000, a tearful announcer on Syria's state-controlled television said that "sadness is in the heart of every man, woman and child." Privately, it was not a sentiment I could share.

"The legacy of his accomplishments and ideas," the announcer continued, "is a planet that will shine not just on this generation, but also on coming generations." Syria's leadership passed on to the next generation of the Assad family, Hafez's son Bashar, then 34. On the day of his father's death, the Syrian parliament passed a constitutional amendment that lowered the minimum age for presidential candidates from 40 to 34. Bashar ran unopposed.

His father left him a legacy as a brilliant tactician, a master of political intrigue, and a Grand Master of the Middle East game of marrying, and divorcing, for convenience. Early in his long tenure, Assad entered a union with Iraq, run by a man he detested personally, Saddam Hussein. The "united" country was meant to underscore solidarity in the fight against Israel, the common enemy. The union did not last. Neither did a later pact with Iran, to counter Iraq.

Publicly, Syria described itself as "the beating heart of Arabism," a champion of pan-Arabism and the Palestinian cause. But when Lebanon disintegrated in sectarian strife, Syria intervened in the civil war on the side of the Christian minority against the Palestinians.

Strategically, Hafez al-Assad achieved little, apart from preventing Syria, ethnically as divided as Lebanon, from sliding into civil war. He failed in his declared ambition to regain the Golan Heights, lost to Israel in the 1967 Arab-Israeli war when he was Syrian defense minister. He did not manage to turn Syria into the regional superpower he thought it should be.

And he never considered making a bold gesture to Israel, as did Egypt's Anwar Sadat, his ally in the 1967 and 1973 Middle East wars. In the autumn of 1977, Sadat asked Assad whether he would accompany him to Jerusalem to make peace with Israel. Assad declined, prompting his Egyptian colleague to call him a "dwarf."

Assad lived on for another 23 years at the helm of his country. Sadat was gunned down by Muslim fundamentalists four years after his trip to Jerusalem.

## Benjamin Netanyahu

## Howard Goller

While prime minister, Benjamin Netanyahu was both hated by former allies who called him a liar and haunted by an inherited peace deal he detested. But time and again the man known by friend and foe alike as Bibi managed to turn the attacks of political adversaries to partisan gain. I interviewed him several times, once only days after Prime Minister Yitzhak Rabin's assassination in November 1995. Opinion polls showed that Netanyahu, then the opposition Likud party leader, didn't have a chance at winning the top office. Rabin's widow, Leah, accused him at the time of fostering a climate of hatred that prompted a right-wing religious Jew to kill her husband. "We have a saying, 'You don't judge a person in his grief'" was what he told me. He called Rabin a Jewish patriot and branded the killing a national tragedy. He complained of a "witch-hunt" aimed at discrediting the opposition. He said the future of the country would be decided at the ballot box, and seven months later he had been elected prime minister.

A square-jawed verbal prizefighter, Netanyahu came to prominence as the younger brother of an Israeli war hero. His brother, Yonatan, known as Yoni, was killed leading the 1976 commando raid on Entebbe, which successfully

Kevin Lamarque

Former Israeli Prime Minister Benjamin Netanyahu speaks to U.S. senators on Capitol Hill in Washington, D.C., April 10, 2002.

freed more than 100 hostages held by members of a Palestinian guerrilla group. Benjamin Netanyahu made his name while Israel's ambassador to the United Nations and later as Israel's spokesman during the Gulf War and at groundbreaking peace talks in Madrid. Born in Israel and educated in the United States, he brought an American campaign style to a country that had been led by grizzled

149

Eastern European-born politicians and Rabin, a taciturn former general. After Rabin's assassination, Netanyahu seized on a wave of suicide bombings as proof the Palestinians could not be trusted. He ousted Nobel peace laureate Shimon Peres as prime minister by a mere 30,000 votes in a May 1996 election. Elected on a peace-with-security platform, Netanyahu redrew Israel's political map as the first Likud leader to give Palestinians a part of the West Bank, territory his rightist party had vowed never to give up. Israelis left, right and center praised him as a pragmatist. Hard-liners accused him of betrayal, having negotiated with Yasser Arafat, long branded a terrorist, and ceded part of Hebron, a sacred West Bank town they said was part of the Greater Israel that God gave the Jews.

Soon after coming to power, Netanyahu headed to the United States to be received by a cheering U.S. Congress. His telegenic looks and soundbite skills made him a welcome spokesman for Israel, America's closest Middle East ally. The reception in Washington seemed a far cry from the isolation Netanyahu faced following Rabin's assassination. Netanyahu pledged allegiance to existing peace deals, but the United States had trouble building trust between him and Arafat. When Netanyahu opened a tourist tunnel near a Muslim shrine in Arab East Jerusalem, Israeli and Palestinian security forces became embroiled in unprecedented gunbattles. He gave the green light to break ground for the Har Homa Jewish settlement on the Jabal Abu Ghneim hilltop at the edge of Jerusalem, plunging peacemaking into a crisis that lasted 19 months.

A former Israeli army commando, Netanyahu laid claim to having reduced attacks on Israel while in office, but this largely deprived Arafat of any credit. A botched Israeli assassination attempt on an Islamic militant from the Hamas group harmed ties with Jordan, long Israel's friendliest Arab peace partner. Relatively new to government, Netanyahu nearly got indicted for corruption. Having put his family in the limelight, he paid for it when his wife fired their boys' nanny, igniting a media frenzy. Yet even when down, Netanyahu never seemed out. After losing to former general Ehud Barak in 1999, Netanyahu said he was taking a political "time-out." But few Israelis doubted that Bibi would vie for a place on Israel's political stage for years to come.

# Hosni Mubarak

## Jonathan Wright

Hosni Mubarak came to power in national trauma but, with a steady hand and extreme caution, he kept Egypt out of major conflict in a dangerous region through more than 20 years.

I was there with my colleague David Rogers when Mubarak, sitting next to President Anwar Sadat at an armed forces parade on October 6, 1981, took a bullet through his military cap as militant Islamists with Kalashnikovs emptied their magazines into Sadat's body beside him.

We didn't see much in the chaos that ensued, between chairs tumbling down the grandstand, the panic of the crowds fleeing for their lives and the roar of the Phantom jets that kept to their scheduled display regardless of the slaughter.

Mubarak appeared on television hours later, his right hand bandaged, a reassuring presence trying to calm the nation.

"The tongue becomes paralyzed, my feelings choke as I mourn the hero of war and peace," he told Egyptians.

Jim Hollander

Egyptian President Hosni Mubarak, host of the Sharm el-Sheikh summit, gestures from inside his limousine as he leaves a Red Sea resort hotel, October 17, 2000.

He inherited a country racked with debt, riven with dissent over Sadat's foreign policies, cut off from its traditional Arab allies and dependent for its next meal on U.S. wheat supplied on credit.

In a country where political longevity is traditional, Mubarak has stayed in power longer than both his predecessors—the revolutionary Gamal Abdel Nasser and the flamboyant Sadat, who made peace with Israel.

By avoiding Nasser's costly adventures and Sadat's confrontational rhetoric, he has given Egypt a measure of economic stability and restored its regional leadership.

But he has been slower to allow political change in a country where the powerful state continues to play much the same central role as it did in the time of the Pharaohs.

His security forces crushed a long and bloody Islamist insurgency in the 1990s but, in the absence of channels for dissent, the risk of militant violence continued to hang over the country.

In a reminder of the 1981 assassination of Sadat, Islamist militants attacked Mubarak's motorcade in the Ethiopian capital Addis Ababa in 1995. His armored car saved him from death.

Mubarak's reaction to the attack was typical of the man—stoical, even fatalistic. "I was cool all the time. There is a God and no one is going to live longer than he has been given to live," he told reporters when he landed back in Egypt.

On the international stage, Mubarak retained the close ties Sadat forged with the United States but slowly mended Egypt's fences with Arab countries that turned their back on Sadat.

He kept Egypt's side of the bargain it made with Israel in the 1979 peace treaty, using his contacts with the Jewish state to promote Palestinian interests and acting as a mentor to Palestinian President Yasser Arafat.

Personally deceived by President Saddam Hussein of Iraq over preparations for the Iraqi invasion of Kuwait in 1990, he did not hesitate to join the United States and others in the successful military campaign to drive Iraqi forces out.

Widely acclaimed as an advocate of peace between Arabs and Israelis, Mubarak has been a leading force in gradually swinging the Arab world behind recognition of Israel.

But relations with successive Israeli governments have been rocky, dependent largely on their attitude to

Palestinians. Mubarak began his career in the military, since the 1952 revolution the traditional path to political leadership. From modest origins in the Nile Delta, he rose to be air force commander during the Middle East war of October 1973.

After 20 years in office, Mubarak shows no sign that he plans to retire and still has no obvious successor.

## Ehud Barak

### Howard Goller

Some journalists on Prime Minister Ehud Barak's plane called his trip to the United States in November 2000 the flight to nowhere. Others called it the flight from hell. I felt as if his noisy Boeing 707 was going around in circles on a flight path symbolic of Middle East peacemaking.

Away from Israel for only about three days, we spent half our time en route. With a Palestinian uprising raging, peace moves failing, and his political future on the line, Barak was racing across the Atlantic to talks in Washington with U.S. President Bill Clinton and an appointment in Chicago with U.S. Jewish leaders. But the overnight hijacking of a Russian airliner to Israel got in the way. Barak ordered his plane home so he could deal with the drama. We were still in the air hours later when the hijacking ended with a Chechen gunman's peaceful surrender. Barak ordered the plane to turn around and head again to Washington. But his time was running out.

An Israeli war hero, who rose to army chief, Barak may well have launched his most daring commando mission on the peace front where he broke one taboo after another. Officials said he offered up to 95 percent of the West Bank

and Gaza in return for peace with the Palestinians and was prepared to share sovereignty over Jerusalem. Had he closed a deal with Palestinian President Yasser Arafat, Barak would have faced a further challenge selling it to an Israeli public eager to make compromises but still digesting the dizzying change.

With 36 years of military service under his belt, Barak fashioned himself a disciple of soldier-turned-peacemaker Yitzhak Rabin and the heir to his "Mr. Security" nickname. But a self-described non-politician, Barak failed as prime

Jim Hollander

Prime Minister Ehud Barak listens to a debate in a special session of parliament, February 13, 2001.

minister to shake the reputation of a Napoleon-like military man who, shunning any advice other than his own, focused only on peacemaking. Some Israelis saw smugness even in his trademark closed-mouth grin. A relative newcomer to politics, Barak zigzagged on issues, alienating the "everyone" in Israeli society he had promised to serve. A Palestinian Intifada starting in September 2000 sealed his fate. Israelis blamed Arafat. They punished Barak. Israel's biggest winner when he came to power, Barak became its biggest loser when voted out 21 months later.

Israel's most decorated soldier, Barak made his name leading daring missions. Disguised as an airport worker, he took part in the storming of a hijacked Sabena airliner at Israel's Ben-Gurion Airport in 1972. The next year, posing as a woman, he took part in a secret military raid in Beirut in which three PLO leaders were killed. News reports said that in 1988, in an effort to snuff out a nascent Palestinian uprising, Barak planned and commanded a raid on a Tunis

suburb. In the operation, commandos killed Abu Jihad, the PLO military commander believed to be leading the uprising.

Ousted as prime minister by former general Ariel Sharon, Barak left the political stage having made good on the most specific peace pledge of his 1999 election campaign. Barak ended Israel's 22-year occupation of south Lebanon in May 2000, bringing the troops home as promised within a year of taking office. But even that success was tainted. The Israeli retreat turned into an undignified and humiliating scramble and a psychological defeat. Victorious Hizbollah guerrillas said their campaign of hit-and-run raids forced the Israelis to give way.

Barak may have failed in bids to forge peace with Syria and the Palestinians. But with the determination and speed of his commando days, Barak reshaped political debate in Israel forever. Whenever Palestinians complained about the occupation, Israelis accused them of having missed the opportunity to end it with Barak at Camp David.

# Why Diplomacy Failed

## Paul Taylor

> *Everyone knows more or less what the solution is. We know where Z is, but we can't get from A to B.*
>
> Javier Solana, European Union foreign policy chief

To cynics, the Middle East peace process is all process and no peace. Envoys from the United States, the United Nations, Europe and Russia have come and gone over the years, vowing to "move the process forward" or at least to "keep the process alive."

There was the Rogers plan, the Fahd plan, the Reagan plan, and more recently the Mitchell report, the Tenet understandings and Saudi Crown Prince Abdullah's initiative. There have been talks about talks about talks—talks about implementing understandings that could lead to confidence-building measures, which, after a cooling-off period, might lead eventually to substantive negotiations. But still the bloodshed continues. The ability of men of violence or ill will to sabotage any diplomatic effort is one of the enduring features of the Israeli-Palestinian conflict. The spoilers have the upper hand.

When U.S. President George W. Bush took office in January 2001, determined to break with his predecessor's unsuccessful activist diplomacy, his administration briefly banned the term "peace process" from its vocabulary. Secretary of State Colin Powell said it did not seem appropriate to the situation. The State Department office of the special envoy in charge of Middle East peacemaking was disbanded. One year and several hundred dead later, the term was back, as was a new special envoy, this time a retired U.S. Marine Corps general, Anthony Zinni, whose every visit to the region seemed to trigger a fresh spasm of violence by Palestinian militants.

Why has diplomacy failed to achieve in the Israeli-Palestinian dispute what it has achieved in civil and national conflicts from Cambodia to South Africa to the Balkans to Northern Ireland since the end of the Cold War?

Is it because the Holy Land is too small for two deeply hostile peoples to share? Or too holy? Is it due to some insurmountable "clash of civilizations"? Is it because the Palestinians at heart do not accept Israel's right to exist? Or because Israel is determined never to withdraw completely from the West Bank and return to its pre-1967 borders?

Is it because each side believes it will ultimately prevail and that time is on its side? Or because neither has yet reached the point of exhaustion?

Or is there something wrong with the process? Was the step-by-step approach of interim agreements adopted when Israel and the Palestine Liberation Organization negotiated the Oslo peace accords in 1993 flawed, giving saboteurs too much opportunity to destroy trust when the sides were supposed to be building confidence?

Or is it more prosaically because of poor leadership, irresolute mediation, the inability or reluctance of the United States to pressure Israel, and a skewed balance of power that gives one side little incentive to make concessions, while the other has the ability to prevent an unacceptable outcome, but not the means to force an acceptable one?

That imbalance leads the Palestinians to strive constantly to draw in outside mediators and protectors, while Israel doggedly resists "internationalizing" the conflict.

## Defining Moment

For many, the Camp David summit in July 2000 was the defining moment in the failure of diplomacy to settle the Israeli-Palestinian conflict. The leaders of the United States, Israel and the Palestinians spent 15 days in seclusion trying to resolve the core issues at the heart of the dispute and failed. Two months later, the second Palestinian Intifada erupted. The guns did the talking.

In the Israeli narrative, diplomacy failed because the Palestinians, as former Israeli Foreign Minister Abba Eban once put it, "never miss an opportunity to miss an opportunity." Presented at Camp David with "the most generous offer Israel has ever made," Palestinian President Yasser Arafat walked away and the Palestinians responded by unleashing an armed insurrection, the Israelis say.

The marathon negotiations mediated by former U.S. President Bill Clinton took place at the hilltop presidential retreat in Maryland, north of Washington, where an earlier generation of Israeli and Egyptian leaders had sealed the

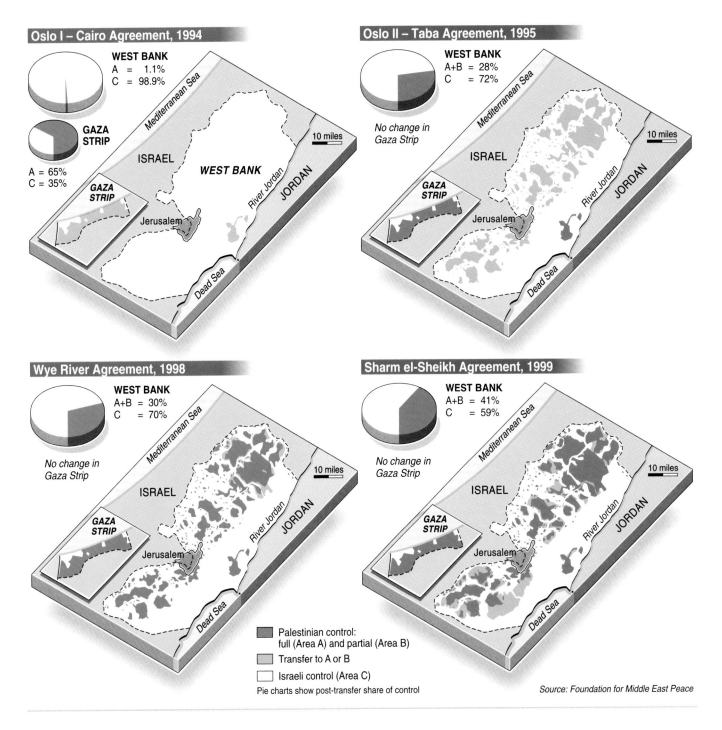

Oslo I – Cairo Agreement, 1994

**WEST BANK**
A  =  1.1%
C  =  98.9%

**GAZA STRIP**
A = 65%
C = 35%

Oslo II – Taba Agreement, 1995

**WEST BANK**
A+B = 28%
C   = 72%

*No change in Gaza Strip*

Wye River Agreement, 1998

**WEST BANK**
A+B = 30%
C   = 70%

*No change in Gaza Strip*

Sharm el-Sheikh Agreement, 1999

**WEST BANK**
A+B = 41%
C   = 59%

*No change in Gaza Strip*

Palestinian control: full (Area A) and partial (Area B)

Transfer to A or B

Israeli control (Area C)

Pie charts show post-transfer share of control

*Source: Foundation for Middle East Peace*

first and most enduring Middle East peace accord in 1978. The second Camp David was the first serious effort to resolve the intractable so-called final status questions of borders, refugees, settlements, Jerusalem and Palestinian statehood that had deliberately been left till the end when Israel and the PLO negotiated the Oslo peace accords.

Underlining their contention that the Palestinians have never really accepted Israel's existence, the Israelis say the summit foundered because Arafat held out for the right of millions of refugees to return to their homes in what is now Israel. That would have radically altered the ethnic balance and undermined the nature of the Jewish state. Arafat also demanded undivided Palestinian sovereignty over the holy places in Jerusalem's walled Old City that Muslims call the Haram al-Sharif (Noble Sanctuary) and Jews call the Temple Mount. The compound houses the Dome of the Rock and al-Aqsa mosque, one of Islam's holiest shrines. To Jews, it is the site of the biblical Temple, and they have made the still-standing Western Wall of this compound their principal prayer site.

The Palestinian narrative is radically different. In their account, Arafat was dragged against his will to an ill-prepared summit called because of the Israeli and American political timetable. There he was subjected to intense pressure to renounce Palestinian rights enshrined in United Nations resolutions. The Palestinians say Israeli Prime Minister Ehud Barak, whose governing coalition was falling apart even before he got to Camp David, never actually put on the table the "most generous offer Israel has ever made," but created a public impression that he was willing to make far-reaching concessions, while skillfully glossing over the tricky small print.

For example, Palestinians say, Barak indicated he could concede sovereignty over the Jordan Valley but demanded that the Israeli army lease back the area for a lengthy period. He insisted on maintaining the main Jewish settlements in the West Bank and sought a six-year transition period to dismantle even the most bitterly contested small ones, such as the heavily guarded cluster of Israeli homes in the center of Hebron—a permanent point of friction in the heart of an Arab city. He offered the Palestinians at most "control" rather than sovereignty in parts of Arab East Jerusalem.

There has been no definitive U.S. account of the talks. Clinton publicly praised Barak afterward for his "creativity" and implied that Arafat had not shown equal vision or flexibility. But some former Clinton aides have suggested Barak shared some blame, both for his high-handed, take-it-or-leave-it approach to the Palestinians, and for his earlier failure to implement agreed withdrawals from the West Bank on time.

Even after the outbreak of the second Intifada, Israeli and Palestinian negotiators continued to meet and advance on what was discussed at Camp David. They reached a series of incomplete understandings at talks in Taba, in the Egyptian Sinai, in January 2001. But Arafat did not embrace the outcome wholeheartedly, and by then Barak, his public legitimacy in Israel ebbing, was a few weeks away from being trounced in a prime ministerial election by hard-liner Ariel Sharon.

When Clinton put forward his own proposals for an Israeli-Palestinian peace settlement in the dying days of his presidency, neither side unconditionally said "yes." But Barak's crumbling government was more enthusiastic than the Palestinians.

Clinton suggested that Israel should annex some 4 percent of the West Bank, containing about 80 percent of the Jewish settlers, and compensate the Palestinians by handing over a smaller area of sovereign Israeli territory. Jerusalem would be the undivided capital of two states. Arab neighborhoods would be Palestinian and Jewish areas Israeli, including settlement neighborhoods built on land annexed in 1967. Each state would have sovereignty over its holy sites in the Old City—the Palestinians over the Haram al-Sharif and the Church of the Holy Sepulchre, and the Israelis over the Western Wall. Neither could excavate beneath the Haram or behind the Wall.

The Palestinian state would be demilitarized and Israel would retain the right to deploy forces on Palestinian territory in a national emergency. An international force, including U.S. troops, would supervise the gradual implementation of an accord.

Clinton proposed that refugees should have the right to return to the state of Palestine but no specific right to return to what is now Israel. They would receive compensation and the possibility of resettlement elsewhere.

Much has been written about why—and even whether—Arafat rejected the proposals. Palestinian scholars say he could not betray the refugees by signing an "end of conflict" agreement without a meaningful right of return. Israeli officials who were involved in the talks say Arafat never fully engaged and always maintained an ambivalence about whether he was a head of state or the leader of a revolutionary movement. Arab leaders, possibly fearing the impact of sympathy for the Palestinians in their own streets, did nothing publicly to encourage him to accept a compromise. Clinton had not mobilized pro-Western Arab leaders before the summit to back a deal.

When the talks ran into trouble and he began calling them, he got little help.

Many outside observers, including Europeans regarded as pro-Palestinian, say Arafat squandered a historic opportunity at Camp David and Taba. "Arafat was wrong not to accept it—clearly wrong—and he has paid so heavily for his mistake," European Commission President Romano Prodi said in April 2002. Palestinians are equally adamant that Arafat was right to reject what in their eyes would have been a sell-out.

Once Sharon and Bush took office, it was clear there would be no way back. Despite Palestinian demands that fresh talks resume where the Taba negotiations left off, each new diplomatic effort since then has begun from a lower starting point.

On both the Israeli and Palestinian sides, the self-proclaimed "peace camp" lost ground in public opinion. The new heroes were suicide bombers or commandos, not the secret negotiators of the Oslo accords.

## Diplomacy's Record

Not that diplomacy has achieved nothing in the Middle East. After President Anwar al-Sadat's bold initiative of traveling to Jerusalem in 1977, Israel and Egypt achieved a peace that has lasted more than a generation, despite wars elsewhere in the region and two Palestinian uprisings against Israeli occupation. Israel may be reviled on the streets of Cairo and denounced daily in the state-controlled Egyptian press, but it still has an embassy in the heart of a city that regards itself as the capital of the Arab world. After the second Intifada erupted, Sadat's successor, President Hosni Mubarak, symbolically recalled his ambassador from Tel Aviv. But he was quick to dismiss talk of an Arab-Israeli war and to rule out any total breach with Israel.

Secretary of State Henry Kissinger began that rapprochement when he shuttled between Cairo and Jerusalem after the 1973 Middle East war to arrange the disengagement of Israeli and Egyptian forces in the Sinai peninsula and across the Suez Canal, a precursor to later peace accords. The United States had backed Egypt diplomatically in 1956, forcing Britain, France and Israel to withdraw after they intervened militarily against President Gamal Abdel Nasser's nationalization of the Suez Canal. But Nasser turned to Moscow for arms and Washington backed Israel in the 1967 Middle East war. Now U.S. engagement in brokering the Sinai deal helped draw Sadat into the American orbit and break Egypt's link with the Soviet Union.

Israel has always found it easier to deal with Arab states than with the Palestinians, with whom it is fighting for the same narrow sliver of land, about the size of Wales. When Israeli Prime Minister Menachem Begin signed a peace treaty with Egypt in 1979 after intensive mediation by U.S. President Jimmy Carter, he pledged that Israel would grant wide-ranging autonomy to the Palestinians. But the PLO, by joining the rejectionist front of Arab states and instructing local West Bank and Gaza leaders not to cooperate with autonomy, helped ensure Begin never had to honor a promise he probably did not intend to keep. To reassure his nationalist and religious supporters, dismayed at the sight of Jewish settlers being forcibly uprooted from the Sinai, Begin allowed Ariel Sharon to embark on an intensive settlement building program in the occupied territories. The United States condemned it but did nothing serious to halt it.

Then in 1982, Begin authorized Sharon, as defense minister, to invade Lebanon, ostensibly to drive Palestinian guerrillas out of rocket-range of Israel's northern border. In fact Israeli troops marched to Beirut in a bid to destroy the PLO and install a friendly Lebanese government. International outrage and American diplomacy helped save Arafat after a 10-week siege in Beirut. Sharon's dream of changing the balance of power in Beirut came to naught with the assassination of Israeli-backed president-elect Bashir Gemayel. The following year, the Israelis withdrew to a southern Lebanon border zone, but occasional rocket attacks against their northern towns and villages continued as Islamic militants of the Hizbollah movement backed by Iran moved into the areas evacuated by the PLO. Resistance to the Israeli invasion unleashed a new weapon on the Middle East stage—suicide bombings.

By this time, a new U.S. administration headed by President Ronald Reagan had taken office. Reagan saw the Middle East conflict through the prism of the Cold War against the Soviet Union, which he branded an "evil empire." To many observers, that priority, rather than the purported power of the pro-Israel lobby in Washington, explained American indulgence toward Israel's Lebanon invasion. The United States and Israel were discussing "strategic cooperation." Begin agreed to let Washington pre-position military equipment in the Jewish state for the U.S. Rapid Deployment Force designed to counter any threat to Western oil supplies in the Gulf.

Viewing Israel as a vital strategic asset made it hard for Reagan to use U.S. leverage effectively to persuade Begin and his more recalcitrant successor, Yitzhak Shamir, to stop building settlements, withdraw from southern Lebanon or move toward negotiations with the Palestinians. Washington did withhold some modern weaponry and satellite imagery from Israel for a while, but the Israelis proved increasingly adept at playing Congress off against the administration whenever pressure was applied.

The outbreak of the first Intifada in December 1987, which took the PLO leadership exiled in Tunis as much by surprise as the Israelis, led Arafat to proclaim the symbolic establishment of a Palestinian state the following year, and to accept U.N. Security Council Resolutions 242 and 338 as the basis for a peace settlement and renounce "all forms of terrorism." Despite Israeli objections, the United States responded by recognizing the PLO and starting a low-level dialogue with Arafat. It was another five years before Israel was ready to talk to its nemesis.

Over the decades, Israel's power to mobilize political support in the United States has grown, to the point where recent former White House aides say it is a major factor in National Security Council deliberations on the peace process. Only the United States, the world's pre-eminent military power, has real leverage in the Middle East. But both U.S. and Israeli domestic politics limit the extent to which it can be used. The notion, widely believed in Europe and the Arab world, that Washington could "deliver" Israel to a peace settlement against its will if an American president really used his power is, former Clinton aides insist, a fantasy.

Succeeding Reagan in 1989, the first President George Bush did play hardball effectively to bring a reluctant Shamir to the Madrid Middle East Peace Conference in 1991 in the wake of the Gulf War. He withheld $10 billion in loan guarantees for Israel to build urgently needed housing for Russian Jewish immigrants to ensure Shamir showed up. But the Israelis were able to impose a diplomatic setup under which Palestinian delegates from the West Bank and Gaza attended only as part of a joint delegation with Jordan. The PLO, ostracized because of its support for Iraqi President Saddam Hussein, was denied any overt role.

Struggling to overcome an economic recession, Bush lost the subsequent election to Clinton. The defeat left a lingering belief among some U.S. political analysts that Bush fell victim to the powerful pro-Israel lobby. Shamir, who also was defeated in 1992, later said he would have dragged the Madrid process out for a decade and given nothing had he remained Israel's leader.

Significantly, the key diplomatic breakthrough in the Israeli-Palestinian conflict took place behind the back of the United States. Israeli negotiators close to Foreign Minister Shimon Peres conducted secret negotiations with PLO representatives in Norway in August 1993, leading to the Oslo accords. Clinton was only informed at the last minute and quickly agreed to give the effort his wholehearted support.

For a while, it looked as if the Oslo agreement would unblock the whole Middle East chessboard. Syria, which had always assumed that neither the Palestinians nor Jordan would dare make peace with Israel without Damascus' agreement, suddenly found itself isolated, weakened by the demise of its Soviet patron and facing a radically altered strategic balance.

That equilibrium tilted further when Israeli Prime Minister Yitzhak Rabin signed a peace treaty with Jordan in 1994 after the Oslo accords had cleared the way for King Hussein to go public with the best-known secret in the Middle East—the close and dependent relationship between the Hashemite monarchy and the Jewish state. Israel's close military alliance with Turkey added to the pressure on Damascus, heightening Syrian fears of encirclement.

Syria and Israel came to the brink of peace in March 2000. A summit between Clinton and ailing Syrian President Hafez al-Assad ended in failure. The Israelis insisted they would only withdraw to a border line traced by colonial powers Britain and France in 1923, set back from the Sea of Galilee. But Damascus said it was entitled to a further strip it held before the 1967 war. Barak said no, as this would have put Syria on the shore of the lake. The two sides missed peace by a few hundred yards.

After that, Barak unilaterally withdrew Israeli forces from southern Lebanon after two decades of costly engagement in the Lebanese quagmire. But Syria and Lebanon's Iranian-backed Hizbollah militia kept the border conflict alive by arguing that Israel should also withdraw from an area known as the Shebaa Farms, which it captured from Syria in the 1967 Middle East war, but which Lebanon now claimed. The United Nations said Israel had complied with a 1978 Security Council resolution calling for its full withdrawal from Lebanon.

Barak turned his attention to seeking a final settlement with the Palestinians only after the failure of his bid with Syria. That repeated a familiar pattern in Israeli diplomacy, in which each successive leader has tried to cut deals with Arab states to remove them from the military equation and isolate the Palestinians. Israeli leaders long believed that the Arab states were the real "problem." If they could be neutralized—by diplomacy if possible, by war if necessary—the Palestinian problem could be "managed." Rabin came to realize that the Palestinians were the central "problem" when he faced the first Palestinian uprising as defense minister in 1987 to 1990.

He died for that belief when a religious Israeli rightist shot him in 1995.

## Disenchantment Sets In

By the lead-up to Camp David in 2000, both sides were thoroughly disenchanted with the Oslo peace process, born amid such high hopes when Rabin and Arafat shook hands on the White House lawn on that sunny day in September 1993.

After decades of decrying the PLO as a "terrorist organization" and convincing themselves they could solve the problem by granting limited autonomy to Palestinian "notables" in the West Bank and Gaza Strip, the Israelis had finally accepted that Arafat was the only man who could deliver a peace deal. But both sides maintained an ambiguous view of the historic bargain of mutual recognition. The Israelis put off all the difficult issues until the end of a multistage peace process, and Rabin quickly began saying that deadlines were not sacred. The pace of Israeli settlement and road building in the West Bank continued apace. Israel's Peace Now movement said that from Oslo until Barak went to Camp David, there was a 53 percent growth in the number of housing units in Jewish settlements.

The Palestinians' attitude toward violence remained deeply ambivalent. Islamic militant groups Hamas and the smaller Islamic Jihad conducted periodic attacks, including suicide bombings, against Israeli targets, often civilians. Arafat's Palestinian Authority, which created no fewer than nine security services, alternated between cracking down on the militants and giving them a free hand in the name of national unity. The Israelis demonized Hamas and demanded that Arafat arrest its activists, helping to undermine any possibility of the Islamic movement being integrated into the Palestinian body politic as a loyal opposition.

Palestinians frequently warned the Israelis that if they did not reach a settlement with the secular Old Guard of the PLO, who had accepted a two-state solution in which the Palestinians would get barely 22 percent of Palestine, the Islamic militants who rejected any compromise would gain the upper hand. As Palestinian political scientist Khalil Shikaki put it, the choice was "peace now or Hamas later."

A wave of Hamas suicide bombings in 1996 catapulted hard-line Likud leader Benjamin Netanyahu to power in an upset victory over Rabin's successor, Shimon Peres. Netanyahu set about lowering Palestinian expectations, further delaying Israeli withdrawals agreed to under the Oslo framework. But after making himself so unpopular with Clinton that he became *persona non grata* at the White House, Netanyahu eventually reached the 1998 Wye Plantation agreement with Arafat, promising a further partial Israeli withdrawal on the West Bank and negotiations for a final status settlement in exchange for greater Palestinian security cooperation. Israel's parliament turned on him, bringing elections forward in a vote that united rightists angry at Netanyahu for signing the deal and leftists angry at him for subsequently freezing it. The dovish Barak won a landslide victory in the nationwide vote and came to power with a mandate for peace.

Israelis came to believe they were giving land but getting no security. This was not peace, one common Israeli saying went, but "piece, by piece, by piece." Palestinians, on the other hand, felt the Israelis were playing for time, spinning out the agreed handover of slivers of territory while racing to expand settlements and grab more Arab land to undermine any final settlement.

The approach of each new deadline for a withdrawal or a negotiating session gave the bombers and radical settlers opportunities to deal fresh blows to the peace process. Far from building confidence, gradualism undermined faith on both sides.

So was it a fatally flawed process, or a failure of political leadership, or of American mediation, or all three? Or is the Israeli-Palestinian conflict inherently insoluble because there is no halfway point between the two sides' historical narratives, religious expectations and political bottom lines?

European Union foreign policy chief Javier Solana, one of the diplomats who has worked alongside the United States since the outbreak of the second Intifada to seek a way out of the crisis, believes the problem is not the ultimate solution but the process. "Everyone knows more or less what the solution is. We know where Z is, but we can't get from A to B," Solana says. What is needed is a short process starting with the establishment of a Palestinian state before a final settlement guaranteed by an international presence on the ground.

The Bush administration's initial withdrawal from a mediating role in 2001 opened the way for other actors, notably the European Union, to try their hand. But none has had much success. The 15-nation EU is Israel's biggest trade partner and the Palestinians' biggest aid donor. Yet it has failed to translate those relationships into political influence because it lacks military clout and its foreign policy is made by a process that often produces hollow declarations and lowest-common-denominator decisions.

Moscow, which was nominally a co-sponsor of the 1991 Madrid peace conference, no longer arms or aids client states in the region, reducing its role to that of a supporting actor for U.S. diplomacy, giving Arab states occasional political cover. The United Nations, long discredited in Israeli eyes as irremediably biased toward the Arabs, despite its historic role in the creation of the Jewish state, is only a bit player when it suits the Israelis, as in southern Lebanon.

Since the September 11, 2001, suicide attacks blamed by the United States on Islamic militants loyal to Saudi exile Osama bin Laden, an additional factor has entered the diplomatic equation that could make the conflict still more difficult to resolve—the primacy of the "war against terrorism" in U.S. thinking. Sharon systematically used the terminology to brand his adversaries terrorists, equating Arafat with bin Laden and refusing to have any dealings with him. A wave of suicide bombings and other attacks in early 2002 that killed 119 Israelis in March alone had a strong impact on U.S. public opinion. Israel's supporters amplified his message powerfully in a congressional election year. Faced with U.S. pressure to attend a new international peace conference, Sharon fought to persuade Washington that Arafat was "the master terrorist" and no partner for peace, seeking to tie him to an attempt to smuggle a shipload of weaponry from Iran and to the suicide bombing campaign.

After initially eschewing such comparisons, influential Bush administration officials, including the president himself, appeared increasingly to view the Israeli-Palestinian conflict primarily as a "terrorism" problem rather than a contest between two national movements or a struggle to end occupation.

Were that view to prevail in Washington, the chances of any diplomatic solution to the conflict would be even more remote.

At a White House ceremony hosted by President Bill Clinton, July 25, 1994, Israeli Prime Minister Yitzhak Rabin (right) and Jordan's King Hussein shake hands over documents on a table ending 46 years of hostility.

President Bill Clinton watches as Israeli Prime Minister Yitzhak Rabin (left) and PLO Chairman Yasser Arafat sign an accord at the White House, September 28, 1995, establishing Palestinian self-rule in most of the West Bank. Behind Rabin and Clinton are King Hussein of Jordan (left), Egyptian President Hosni Mubarak and aides.

Gary Hershorn

President Bill Clinton (front, second right), flanked by his wife Hillary, bows his head as he pays his respects to assassinated Prime Minister Yitzhak Rabin at Mt. Herzl Cemetery in Jerusalem, November 6, 1995. Former Presidents Jimmy Carter (left) and George Bush are part of the U.S. delegation.

David Silverman

A Palestinian throws a rock at Israeli
soldiers during fierce clashes in the
West Bank city of Hebron,
March 22, 1997.

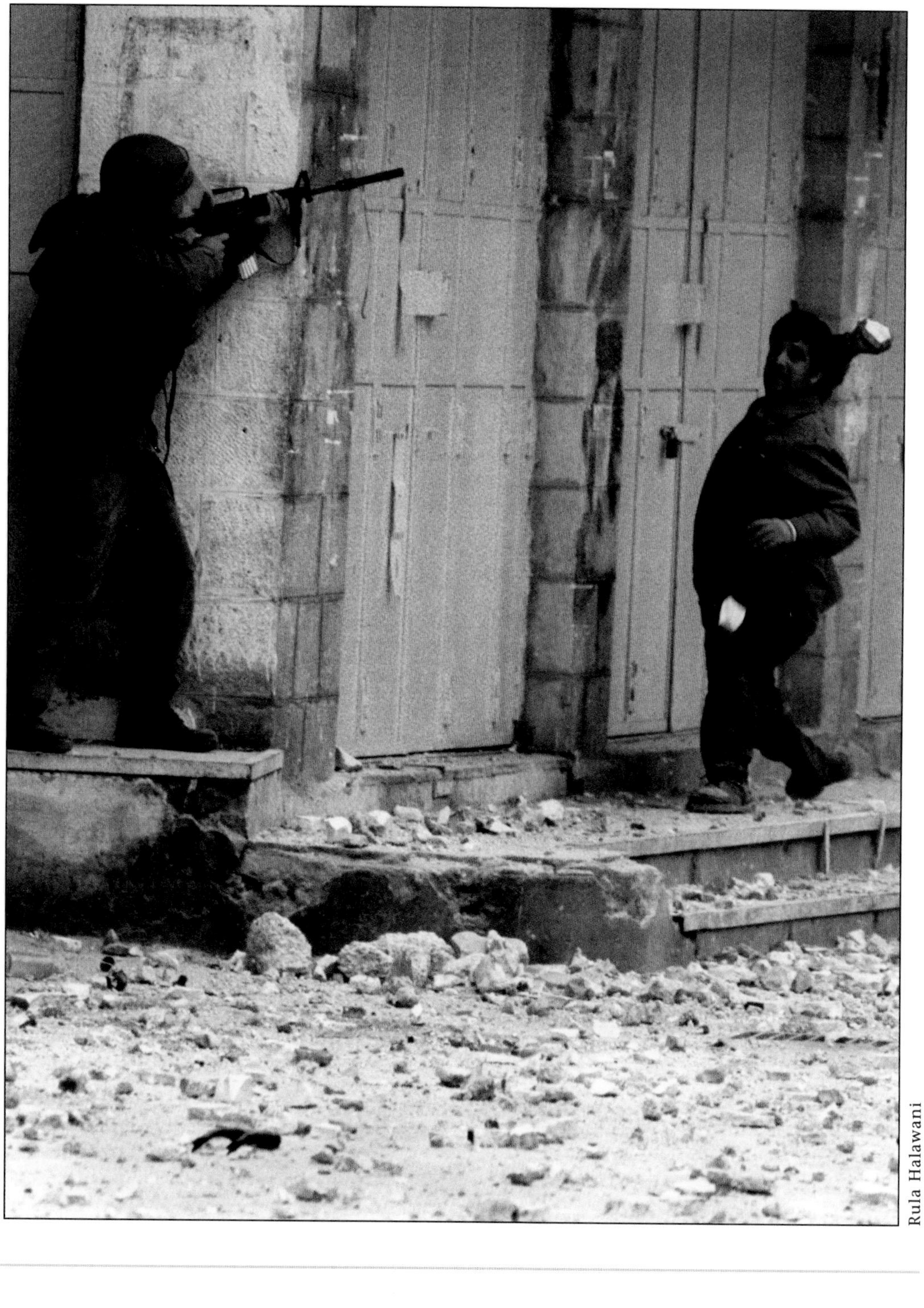

Rula Halawani

Win McNamee

Palestinian President Yasser Arafat kisses the hand of Leah Rabin, widow of slain Israeli Prime Minister Yitzhak Rabin, after speaking at the Commemoration of Yitzhak Rabin in Oslo's City Hall, November 2, 1999.

Larry Rubenstein

President Bill Clinton, Israeli Prime Minister Benjamin Netanyahu (right) and
Palestinian President Yasser Arafat (left) leave the Rose Garden of the White House
arm-in-arm, October 15, 1998, after a statement on the start of peace talks at the
secluded Wye River Plantation.

**Gary Hershorn, December 1998**

When I took this picture, I felt I was recording an extraordinary triumph of modern diplomacy. Two leaders, known for their vibrant emotions, were sealing a deal which everyone hoped one day would be seen as a landmark toward peace.

I had traveled with President Bill Clinton to the Middle East, knowing the highlight of his trip was to be at the Palestine National Council meeting in Gaza, where Yasser Arafat would call for a vote to abolish from the Palestinian Charter all references to the destruction of Israel.

The White House press corps was driven by bus to Gaza from Jerusalem. Our first stop was the new Gaza International Airport, where the two leaders cut a ribbon to open it. On our way to the council meeting, having never traveled in Gaza before, I remember being struck by the beautiful sand and sea of the coastline.

After lengthy security checks, we took our positions close to Clinton and Arafat, who were on a platform. The meeting was packed with delegates awaiting Arafat's words. At the end of the speech Arafat did indeed ask for a vote, and in a show of hands delegates clearly voted to remove the destruction of Israel clauses from their charter.

Clinton rose from his seat on the podium, walked over to Arafat, and they clasped each others' hands. Arafat seemed to be thanking Clinton by holding the president's hand to his heart. The president had a look of solemn satisfaction that Arafat had delivered.

Gary Hershorn

White House photo

President Bill Clinton (left) and Vice President Al Gore (right) walk with Palestinian leader Yasser Arafat and Secretary of State Madeleine Albright (center) at Wye River Plantation in Maryland, October 18, 1998.

White House photo

President Bill Clinton in a private moment with Israeli Prime Minister Benjamin Netanyahu on the back porch of the River House at the Wye River Plantation in Maryland, October 17, 1998.

A Palestinian youth is dragged from his home in Khan Younis in the southern Gaza Strip by Israeli soldiers in the first Intifada, or Palestinian uprising, December 14, 1987.

Jim Hollander

Israeli Prime Minister Benjamin Netanyahu (right) shakes hands with Palestinian President Yasser Arafat (left) as President Bill Clinton and King Hussein watch after the formal signing ceremony for a land-for-security deal, October 23, 1998.

White House photo

President Bill Clinton meets with Israeli Prime Minister Ehud Barak and Palestinian
President Yasser Arafat, July 25, 2000, at Camp David near Thurmont, Maryland.
The Camp David Middle East peace summit collapsed after 15 days of intense
negotiations.

Israeli Prime Minister Ehud Barak (right) playfully pushes Palestinian President Yasser Arafat (center) into the Laurel cabin on the grounds of Camp David as President Bill Clinton watches, during peace talks, July 11, 2000. Arafat and Barak were each insisting that the other proceed through the door first.

Win McNamee

A kneeling Israeli soldier takes aim as a Palestinian woman hurls a rock at close range during demonstrations in the village of Burin, outside Nablus on the West Bank, February 29, 1988.

Jim Hollander

Palestinian President Yasser Arafat (right) looks George Mitchell, a former U.S. senator turned peace envoy, in the eye after a news conference in Gaza, December 11, 2000.

Jerry Lampen

Jim Hollander

Prime Minister Ehud Barak (center) smiles as he and members of the U.S.-led fact-finding commission to the Middle East headed by former Senator George Mitchell (left) and Norwegian Foreign Minister Thorbjoern Jagland (right) heap their hands together in a multiple handshake in Barak's offices in Jerusalem, December 11, 2000. Reaching in from left but unseen is Javier Solana, European Union foreign policy chief.

Hussein Hussein

Palestinian President Yasser Arafat (left), in a picture handed out by his office, meets with U.S. Secretary of State Colin Powell in Arafat's Ramallah office, April 14, 2002.

A Palestinian woman and an Israeli
soldier exchange glances, December 17,
1987, as he passes her house at the
southernmost part of the Gaza Strip, 10
days after the start of the first Intifada,
or Palestinian uprising against Israeli
occupation.

Jim Hollander

# Jerusalem— Cauldron of Conflict

## Alan Elsner

> *Pray for the peace of Jerusalem; May those who love you prosper.*
>
> Psalms 122:6

The late Israeli poet Yehuda Amichai once wrote that holiness hung in the sky above Jerusalem like industrial pollution over other cities. The air, he said, was "filled with prayers and dreams … hard to breathe." He added that in Jerusalem, "The right to vote is granted even to the dead."

History lives in Jerusalem as in no other city. The rhythms and cadences of the city may alter over time, yet the echoes of the past are still heard. In Jewish neighborhoods on Friday afternoons, an air raid siren announces the beginning of the Sabbath when much of the city shuts down. Two thousand years ago, as reported by the historian Josephus, a trumpeter on the Temple Mount would sound a blast to announce the Sabbath. Now, of course, all too often the Sabbath siren also echoes the screams and wails of fire trucks and ambulances rushing to the scene of the latest act of violence.

There is no consensus on the past in Jerusalem. The warring parties squabble as much over what may or may not have happened 3,000 years ago as they do over what happened last week or what should happen next year. Meron Benvinisti, a former deputy mayor, wrote, "The chronicles of Jerusalem are a gigantic quarry from which each side has mined stones for the construction of its myths—and for throwing at each other."

Jerusalem is a holy city to the three great monotheistic religions—Judaism, Christianity and Islam. For Jews, Jerusalem is the place where King Solomon built the Temple. At the heart of the Temple complex was the Holy of Holies, the only place on Earth where a human stood fully in the presence of God and from which God's presence, they believe, has not departed.

Christians revere Jerusalem as the site of Jesus' crucifixion and resurrection. Rival Christian sects have often fought bitterly for control over the Church of the Holy Sepulcher, built on the traditional site of Golgotha, the place of skulls, where the Romans crucified Jesus, and where he was entombed. In the nineteenth century the French gained from the sultan the right for Catholics to look after the holy places in Jerusalem. The Russian tsar saw this as an affront to the Orthodox Church.

The religious quarrel escalated, giving rise to the Crimean War, which pitted Britain and France against Russia. That tension eventually resolved into a tenuous agreement, known as the Status Quo, in which ownership and cleaning rights of every single object in the church and every inch of its structure are set down. Such rules are observed to this day.

In the twelfth century, fighting among Christian denominations led Muslim conqueror Saladin to give the key to the church to a Muslim family, which to this day holds it.

For Muslims, Jerusalem is called Al Quds, the Holy City. The Temple Mount, which Islam knows as the Haram al-Sharif, or Noble Sanctuary, is their third holiest site, after Mecca and Medina. A 35-acre, not quite rectangular, enclosure on the southeast corner of the Old City, this is surely the most embattled, most fiercely contested plot of land on Earth. So much sanctity in so small a space: it is almost like the compressed energy inside an atom. Any spark can trigger a chain reaction, unleashing enormous destructive force. When adherents of each faith insist that they alone are right, it becomes difficult for them to share such a confined space as good neighbors.

Muslims believe Mohammad had a vision in which he made a supernatural night journey to the city astride a winged beast and then ascended to heaven. The site now contains the silver domed al-Aqsa Mosque and the glorious Dome of the Rock, the city's most recognizable landmark. It is built around the so-called Foundation Stone, a large rock that may have marked the site of the Holy of Holies within the biblical Temple. Over the centuries, more and more traditions have attached themselves to this rock. Some believe that the world itself was created around this rock, that Adam was born here, that Cain and Abel made their sacrifices here and that God called out to Abraham, stopping him from sacrificing Isaac here. Adherents of each faith not only believe that the world was created in Jerusalem but also that it will end there. The dead will rise, humankind will be judged, final battles will be fought, good will conquer evil.

## Jerusalem's holy sites

**①** **Temple Mount** The 35-acre compound is a profound symbol of the Jewish nation and the place where religious Jews believe redemption will take place when the Messiah arrives. The area is also deeply significant to the Palestinians and to Muslims around the world, who know it as Haram al-Sharif (the Noble Sanctuary)

**②** **Dome of the Rock** Islamic tradition says that the Prophet Mohammad ascended to heaven on a winged horse from this spot

**③** **al-Aqsa Mosque** The third holiest site in Islam after Mecca and Medina in Saudi Arabia

**④** **Western Wall** A place of prayer and the main focus of Jewish prayer

**⑤** **Church of the Holy Sepulcher** Christians believe the church marks the site where Jesus Christ was crucified and later resurrected

### Jerusalem's Old City

100 yards

N

Herod's Gate

St.Stephen's Gate

Damascus Gate

Via Dolorosa

Golden Gate

Suqkhan Az-Zeit

MUSLIM QUARTER

Shuk Ha-Basamin

New Gate

CHRISTIAN QUARTER

David

Ha-Shalshelet

Ha-Yehudim

JEWISH QUARTER

Jaffa Gate

Citadel

Dung Gate

ARMENIAN QUARTER

Zion Gate

2 miles

Ramallah

Givon

WEST BANK

Municipal boundary

JERUSALEM
Old City

Maale Adumim

ISRAEL

Abu Dis

Gilo

Bethlehem

"Green line" (1949 Armistice Line)

### Israel's proposal for Jerusalem

The Camp David talks in the United States in July 2000 foundered partly because Israeli and Palestinian negotiators could not reconcile their claims to the holy sites

| | |
|---|---|
| Israeli greater Jerusalem | Current and projected Israeli built-up areas |
| Palestinian Jerusalem | Current and projected Palestinian built-up areas |

In September 2000, Israeli opposition leader **Ariel Sharon** visited the Temple Mount

*Source: Palestinian Academic Society for the Study of International Affairs*

Though most religious Jews believe the Temple will rise again only when the Messiah comes, a small but vociferous group of extreme right-wingers wants to destroy the mosques and begin construction immediately. Some American Christian fundamentalist groups support them out of a belief that rebuilding the Temple is an essential precondition for the Second Coming of Jesus. For Muslims, such words merely confirm their fears that Israel and its American backers intend to throw them off the Haram al-Sharif and raze their holy mosques.

One group of Israeli militants in the early 1980s did develop a detailed plot to blow up the mosques. The group carried out a number of attacks on Palestinian politicians and civilians before being uncovered, arrested and brought to trial by the Israeli authorities. Most drew relatively light sentences or were pardoned and released a few years later.

Despite its blood-drenched history, Jerusalem has stood throughout the centuries as a metaphor of perfection for visionaries and poets of far away who would never set eyes on the city. The nineteenth-century English poet William Blake dreamed of building Jerusalem amid the "dark, satanic mills" of industrial England. In 1832, Joseph Smith, the founder of Mormonism, had a vision in which he was commanded to build a "new Jerusalem" in Independence, Missouri.

To them, Jerusalem symbolized an ideal peace, but the city also has far ghastlier associations. The gates of hell—in Hebrew "Gehenna"—are said to be in the Valley of Hinnom, just outside the city walls in a place once associated with human sacrifice. Formal religious sacrifice may have ended long ago, but the city continues to claim its bloody offerings. Jerusalem has experienced at least 40 wars and sieges in its history.

"It was impossible to look upon the vast numbers of slain without horror. Everywhere lay fragments of human bodies and the very ground was covered by the blood of the slain," wrote William of Tyre, a witness to the slaughter that followed the Crusader conquest of Jerusalem in 1099, when the victorious legions of Christ massacred some 30,000 Muslim and Jewish residents of the city in a killing spree that lasted until there was no one left to kill. Limbs lay rotting in the streets for weeks afterward. Today, in the aftermath of suicide bombings of cafes and restaurants, burial squads collect the body parts immediately.

When a Persian army conquered Jerusalem in 614 B.C., the monk Antiochus Strategos said its soldiers rushed into the city hissing and roaring like wild boars, killing Christian men, women and children—a total, he estimated, of 66,555.

In A.D. 70 when the Romans destroyed the Second Temple, Josephus described the scene in words that still shock: "The Temple Mount, enveloped in flames from top to bottom, appeared to be boiling up from its very roots, yet the sea of flames was nothing to the ocean of blood."

Again Yehuda Amichai said it best: In Jerusalem, he wrote, numbers do not refer to bus routes, as in other cities, but to years in history: "70 after, 1917, 500 B.C., Forty-Eight. These are the lines you really travel on."

If Jerusalem were only about religion, the situation would be difficult enough. But over the centuries, competing nationalist designs have been welded to religious symbols, turning the struggle for control into a clash of nations. In Jerusalem, everything counts. What in other places would be mundane municipal matters, such as the building of roads and hospitals and the laying of water and electricity

THE ISRAELI-PALESTINIAN CONFLICT     crisis in the middle east

lines, in Jerusalem become charged with symbolic, even spiritual, meaning.

The disputes even extend underground. Palestinians accuse Israeli archeologists of burrowing down under their sacred sites to undermine them. Israelis accuse Palestinian archeologists of destroying the rich historical record of Jewish settlement in ancient Jerusalem.

History in Jerusalem has a way of repackaging itself. A political figure decides to pay a visit to the Temple Mount. His arrival sparks a riot among native residents who regard the intruder as foreign and view the incursion as sacrilege as well as a deadly threat to their tenuous control. This happened in the year 180 B.C., when the appearance of a Greek government figure named Heliodorus sparked fury among the beleaguered Jews fighting to hold fast to their holy Temple. It happened again almost 2,200 years later when then-Israeli opposition leader Ariel Sharon decided to pay a symbolic visit to the Temple Mount. The furious reaction among Palestinian Muslims marked the beginning of the al-Aqsa *Intifada*, or second Palestinian uprising.

No group has been spared suffering and bloodshed in Jerusalem, yet members of each group often see their own suffering as special, conferring on them a unique relationship with the city that eclipses all other claims.

When Israel organized in 1995 a celebration marking what it said was the 3,000th anniversary of the establishment of Jerusalem as capital of the Kingdom of Israel, the official program stated: "No other people designated Jerusalem as its capital in such an absolute and binding manner. Jerusalem is the concrete historical expression of the Jewish religion and its heritage on the one hand and the independence and sovereignty of the

Jewish people on the other. Jerusalem's identity as a spiritual and national symbol at one and the same time has forged the unique and eternal bond between this city and the Jewish people, a bond that has no parallel in the annals of the nations."

At the same time, a textbook used in Palestinian schools in the West Bank harks back to the period before King David, when the city was ruled by a Canaanite tribe called the Jebusites: "The Jebusites, a Canaanite people, are the ancestors of the Palestinians. Abraham was neither a Jew nor a Christian but a believer in one God. ... Jerusalem has been the capital of our Palestinian Arab homeland ever since it was built by our ancestors, the Jebusites and the Arab Canaanites, in the heart of *Falastin*. The Arab presence in Jerusalem was never interrupted, in contrast to the Jewish presence, which disappeared."

A leaflet given to tourists by the Waqf, the Islamic religious authority that controls the Haram al-Sharif, questions that a Jewish temple ever stood on the site: "Some believe it was the site of the Temple of Solomon, peace be upon him ... or the site for the Second Temple ... although no documented historical or archaeological evidence exists to support this," the pamphlet states.

Yasser Arafat himself, in front of President Bill Clinton and others at Camp David in 2000, stated that there had never been a Jewish Temple on the Temple Mount. He said whatever Jewish temple might have existed was located in Nablus and Jesus was never in Jerusalem. Bemused American and Israeli negotiators brought in the *Encyclopaedia Britannica* as a "neutral text" to dispute this point, but Arafat remained unconvinced.

For both sides, it seems sometimes that the other does not truly exist. In 1967, a few weeks before the Six-Day War, the Israeli songwriter Naomi Shemer wrote a song, *Jerusalem of Gold*, that remains an Israeli classic.

"Jerusalem of gold, and of bronze and of light. Behold, I am a violin for all your songs," she sang. And in the third verse she sang of the Old City, then ruled by Jordan, from which Jews were barred: "The market place is empty, and no one frequents the Temple Mount."

The phrase "Jerusalem of Gold" is a 2,000-year-old term for a woman's tiara, of the kind a wealthy man might give his bride. Shemer's song implied that the Old City had remained empty since the expulsion of the Jews in 1948 and was waiting for the beloved to return. She was expressing the frustration born of a situation in which Jews were denied access to their holiest site. But in doing so, she simply did not see those who were there.

Just weeks after the song was first performed, Israeli troops captured East Jerusalem. It was the first time Jews had controlled the Old City, including the holy places, since A.D. 70.

Historically, the first archaeological find mentioning the city that would become Jerusalem was an inscription on a shattered Egyptian vase that has been dated to the reign of Pharaoh Sestoris III (1878–1842 B.C.). The city, called *Rushalimum*, was one of 19 Canaanite cities said to be enemies of Egypt. The first biblical mention is in Genesis (14:18–20), when Melchizedek, king of the Canaanite city of *Shalem*, blesses Abraham. Shalem, the Hebrew word at the root of Jerusalem, may have been the name of a Syrian god identified with the evening star or the setting sun. The Hebrew word means "wholeness or perfection." The same word also gives rise to the Hebrew *shalom* and the Arabic *salaam*, meaning peace. Thus Jerusalem is associated both with oneness and with peace—yet it enjoys neither.

The city's real appearance in history began with a political decision when King David conquered the city from the Jebusites and declared it his capital. Striving to unite the tribes of Israel into one kingdom, he carefully selected a site located on the border of the southern and northern tribes but held by neither of them. Similar considerations prompted the selection of Washington, D.C., as capital of the United States many centuries later.

Throughout history, successive rulers sought to impress themselves upon the city through the construction of mighty religious edifices. Thus, David's son, King Solomon, built the first Temple to house the Ark of the Covenant, the dwelling place for the Almighty on Earth. The High Priest, in a state of ritual purity, was the only person allowed to enter the sanctuary once a year on the Day of Atonement. When the city fell to the Babylonians in the year 586 B.C., the Temple was destroyed. But within 60 years Jews were allowed to return, and the Second Temple was dedicated in 520 B.C. This structure was vastly expanded and improved upon five centuries later by King Herod, who built the massive retaining walls, one of which still stands—the Western Wall, constructed of giant slabs weighing up to five tons each. Forbidden to enter the Temple Mount itself for fear of unwittingly desecrating the spot where the Holy of Holies once stood, Jews have made this wall their principal prayer site in the city.

Muslims refer to the Western Wall as *Al Buraq al Sharif* and believe it is the spot where the Prophet tethered his supernatural steed, Buraq, during the night journey. Buraq means "lightning"—as does the Hebrew name of former Israeli Prime Minister Ehud Barak, who made a journey to meet Palestinian leader Yasser Arafat at Camp David in the summer of 2000. Their failure to agree on a final peace settlement of the Israeli-Palestinian conflict set off a new chain of violence that has written yet another horrific chapter in the city's bloody story.

In Jerusalem, buildings have always been political statements. When the Roman Empire adopted Christianity in the fourth century A.D., Christians embarked on a massive church-building program. The edifice now known as the Church of the Holy Sepulcher towered above the desecrated Temple Mount, a physical symbol of Christianity's dominance over Judaism. Jews were forbidden to live in the city, and the site of the former Temple became a garbage dump.

When in A.D. 638 the Caliph Umar conquered the city in the name of Islam, he was horrified to see the centuries of filth that had piled up on the Temple Mount and ordered the site cleared. Half a century later, the magnificent Dome of the Rock rose to challenge the towering Christian churches. A second mosque, the silver-domed al-Aqsa, was built in close proximity.

The inscriptions on the Dome of the Rock were specifically directed at Christians. They proclaim that God is one and never fathered a child. "So believe in God and all the messengers and stop talking about a Trinity."

The transformation of Jerusalem into a sacred place for Muslims evolved through history, legend and faith. The Koran does not explicitly mention Jerusalem by name and never specifically says that Mohammad's night journey was to the city. The text states: "Glorified be He who carried His servant by night from the Holy Mosque to the Farthest Mosque, the precincts whereof we have blessed" (Koran, sura 17:1). The Arabic words for "farthest mosque" are "al-Aqsa," but only after a mosque was built in Jerusalem 68 years after Mohammad's death and named al-Aqsa did the city become associated with the night journey.

When the Crusaders conquered Jerusalem, they placed a giant cross on top of the Dome of the Rock, covered up the inscriptions and turned al-Aqsa into the military headquarters of the Knights Templar, while massively rebuilding the Church of the Holy Sepulcher. But less than 90 years later, the Crusaders were defeated and the city fell back into Muslim hands. Today, some Palestinians look back to the defeat of the Crusaders for inspiration. Choosing to view the Israelis as foreign interlopers, they believe that if only they remain steadfast and patient, the Jews may hold Jerusalem no longer than the Crusader kingdom did.

The first thing the Israelis did on capturing the Old City in 1967 was to tear down all the houses adjacent to the Western Wall, displacing around 600 people, who were given three hours to clear out of their homes. Bulldozers worked all night to level the historic Maghribi quarter, which was transformed into the giant plaza that visitors to the Wall see today. Before that, access to the Wall was on a narrow strip of pavement hemmed in by buildings.

But Defense Minister Moshe Dayan also made the crucial decision that the Haram would remain a Muslim site to be run by Muslims. Jews would be allowed to enter the Temple Mount if they wished but would not be permitted to pray there. For Jewish prayer, the focus would be the Wall. His hope was that with some physical separation, the adherents of both faiths could get along.

For a time this succeeded, but in recent years the clashes have grown more severe and more frequent.

1969: al-Aqsa is set ablaze by Dennis Michael Rohan, a 28-year-old Australian Christian. Psychologists later name this kind of destructive religious fervor the Jerusalem Syndrome. The action sparks riots across the entire Muslim world. Angry protesters accuse Israeli firefighters of spraying gasoline on the flames.

1982: Alan Goodman, an American Israeli inspired by extremist Rabbi Meir Kahane, goes on a shooting rampage on the Temple Mount, killing one and wounding 30. It sets off a week of rioting in Jerusalem and the occupied territories.

1983: Israeli police arrest more than 40 members of a Jewish underground group who were planning to blow up the al-Aqsa and Dome of the Rock mosques.

1990: Israeli police shoot dead 17 Palestinians on the Temple Mount. An Israeli state inquiry finds that Arabs started the clash by stoning Jewish worshippers at the Western Wall below. But an Israeli judge later rules that police bungling, not Arab provocation, ignited the clash when a tear gas grenade fell into a group of Muslim women.

1996: Israeli workmen knock open an ancient tunnel under the Old City that runs adjacent to the Temple Mount. The act, backed by the government, provokes Palestinian protests. Sixty Arabs and 15 Israeli soldiers are killed in the confrontations.

2000: Ariel Sharon visits the Temple Mount accompanied by a heavy security presence. A wave of fury sweeps the territories and the Muslim world. The Second Intifada begins. A few months later, Sharon is elected Israeli prime minister.

After 1967, Israel also embarked on an ambitious building project aimed at solidifying its control over the entire city and cementing a large Jewish majority. New neighborhoods were built on expropriated land, ringing the city with high-rise apartments, encircling Arab enclaves with Jewish suburbs. High-rise office blocks thrust their way into the famous city skyline once dominated by the Dome of the Rock and graceful church spires. On Mount Scopus, they vastly expanded the campus of the Hebrew University. It resembles a kind of modern fortress, bristling with faux towers and fortifications. In doing this, the Israelis were simply following the example of so many of Jerusalem's past rulers.

Yet despite all their efforts, the Israelis failed to truly unite the city. Demographically, they have had some success. Jews have been a majority in Jerusalem since the middle of the 19th century and now comprise about two thirds of the population of about 633,000, even though the Palestinian birthrate continues to exceed the Israeli birthrate. However, politically the Israelis have not succeeded. The two communities remain separate. There is scarcely a mixed street, let alone a mixed neighborhood, in the entire city. The violence that has rocked the city in recent years has only deepened this separation. Jerusalem today is like two separate geographies superimposed one upon the other. How to disentangle them so that both Israelis and Palestinians can establish the city as their functional capitals remains perhaps the greatest challenge to any potential Middle East peacemaker.

If there is one thing to emerge from history, it is that no victory in Jerusalem has been permanent. Today's victors may emerge centuries later as tomorrow's vanquished. There have been a few periods in Jerusalem's history when different groups have managed to coexist and when minorities have been treated with dignity, though rarely if ever as equals. No one can doubt that Jerusalem can and does inspire deep love among its adherents. The question is, can it also inspire tolerance?

Street scene on the Jaffa Road, Jerusalem, in the early days of Israeli nationhood.

Israeli Government Press Office

Moshe Milner

Snow blankets the Temple Mount, known to Muslims as Haram al-Sharif, in the Old
City of Jerusalem, January 1992.

Jim Hollander

Two elderly Palestinian men and an ultra-Orthodox Jewish man with his two sons
pass each other in a market area in Jerusalem's Old City, January 27, 2001.

A Palestinian woman passes an Orthodox Jewish woman praying in an alley of
Jerusalem's Old City, November 3, 2000.

Natalie Behring

Thousands of Jews attend a prayer vigil at Jerusalem's Western Wall, July 11, 2000.

Natalie Behring

A Palestinian woman passes an Israeli border police officer in front of the Haram al-Sharif, or the Temple Mount, in Jerusalem after Friday prayers ended, April 20, 2001.

Reinhard Krause

Reinhard Krause

An Arab shopkeeper waits for customers in the deserted Via Dolorosa in Jerusalem's Old City, the path taken by Jesus to his crucifixion, March 28, 2002. In previous years the narrow roadway would have been packed with pilgrims and tourists.

Jim Hollander

Armed Israeli border police on security duty on the Via Dolorosa as two Palestinians carry large wooden crosses back to the first station of the cross, April 21, 2000.

Jim Hollander

A view of the Tower of David and part of the Old City at the Jaffa Gate area of Jerusalem, spring 1993. Mist fills the area between the Old City and Mount Scopus in the background.

Radu Sigheti

Pope John Paul II sits between Israel's Chief Rabbi Yisrael Meir Lau (left) and Sheikh Tayseer al-Tamimi, a Muslim cleric who left the inter-religious gathering before it ended March 23, 2000, at Jerusalem's Pontifical Institute Notre Dame. Sheikh Tamimi did not shake Rabbi Lau's hand, left the gathering early and did not take part in a symbolic tree planting for peace.

Christian pilgrims reach their arms into a solitary beam of light passing through a window in the Church of the Holy Sepulcher, April 29, 2000, on the Saturday of Lights during the ceremony of Holy Fire.

Evelyn Hockstein

Natalie Behring

An Orthodox Jew silhouetted against the Dome of the Rock in the Old City of
Jerusalem, December 26, 2000.

Pope John Paul II touches the ancient stones of the Western Wall as he prays, March 26, 2000.

Jim Hollander

An ultra-Orthodox Jew prays at the snow-covered Western Wall, January 28, 2000.

Nati Shohat/Flash 90

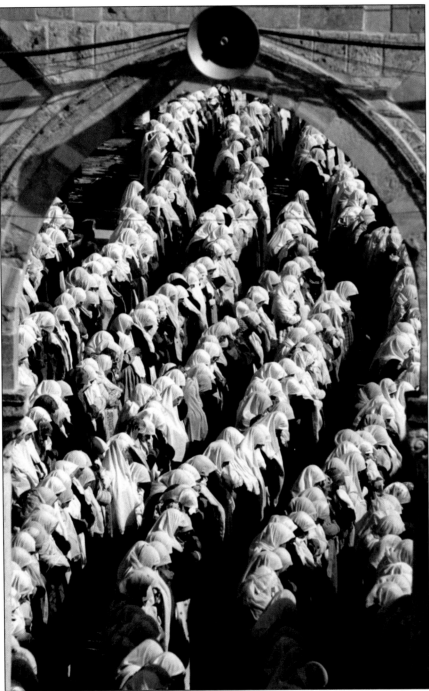

Veiled Palestinian women pray under
one of the ancient arches that decorate
the Temple Mount, known to Muslims
as the Haram al-Sharif,
January 23, 1998.

Nati Shohat/Flash 90

Palestinian girls surround Faisal al-Husseini (center, bottom), then the senior Palestinian official in Jerusalem, as they release scores of white doves, symbolizing peace, on the steps of the Orient House, Jerusalem, March 20, 2000. The Orient House was decorated with dozens of Vatican flags as well as Palestinian flags in preparation for the historic visit to Jerusalem of Pope John Paul II.

Jim Hollander

Natalie Behring

Hundreds of Israelis carry flags as they participate in a rally outside the Old City's Jaffa Gate in Jerusalem, January 8, 2001.

Jim Hollander

An American pilgrim playing the part of Jesus Christ, complete with a crown of thorns and actors' blood make-up, carries his cross on the Via Dolorosa on Good Friday, April 21, 2000, as other pilgrims playing his mother and Roman centurions take part in a re-enactment of the route Jesus took through the Old City.

Palestinians hurl shoes as Israeli police storm the Haram al-Sharif, also known as the Temple Mount, July 29, 2001.

Ammar Awad

An Israeli border police officer and a Palestinian scream at each other in the Old City
of Jerusalem, October 13, 2000.

Natalie Behring

In the West Bank town of Bethlehem, December 24, 2001, a Christian nun walks through the empty nave of the Church of the Nativity, believed to be the site of the birthplace of Jesus.

Jim Hollander

A Christian pilgrim holding candles bows and kisses the 14-point silver star in a marble floor in the tiny grotto within the Church of the Nativity, December 20, 1998.

Jim Hollander

Fire spreads as thousands of Orthodox Christians light candles inside the Church of the Holy Sepulcher surrounding the Tomb of Jesus (center) as the "Ceremony of the Holy Fire" is celebrated, April 29, 2000.

Nuns walk in the empty Church of the Holy Sepulcher in Jerusalem's Old City on Easter Sunday, March 31, 2002, which in previous years attracted thousands of tourists and pilgrims.

Reinhard Krause

**Peter Andrews, December 2000**

This picture of a rainbow arching over Bethlehem captured for me, not only a moment of great beauty, but also a dream I had of visiting the place of Jesus' birth on Christmas Eve. I felt it was even more important to be there at the end of the first year of the new century. But the vision was poignant because times were turbulent, with the Intifada uprising entering its fourth month. Many pilgrims had traveled to Bethlehem despite the roadblocks.

On that day the skies were covered with clouds, but from time to time a beam of light broke through. I felt as if the overcast skies were trying to part and to bring hope from above.

At one moment, outside the Church of the Nativity, my heart leapt at this beautiful ribbon of hope, a rainbow over Bethlehem. I took the picture, but the rainbow did not last long and faded.

Peter Andrews

# Reuters Correspondents, Photographers and Graphic Journalists

### Tsafrir Aboyov

Born in Israel in 1966, Aboyov studied at the Dawson Institute of Photography in Montreal. He has worked since then as a freelance photojournalist—in Los Angeles for Magma agency and news magazine and, since 1996, in Israel for Reuters and the *Yedioth Ahronoth* daily newspaper.

### Wafa Amr

Amr has been based in Jerusalem since 1994 and has covered the major developments in Middle East politics in recent years, including the two Palestinian uprisings and a range of peace talks.

### Khaled al-Hariri

Khaled Hariri, 40, was born in Syria. He has been a photographer with Reuters since 1992.

### Peter Andrews

In 1991 Andrews joined Reuters during the first coup in Moscow. In 1996 he moved to Johannesburg as Chief Photographer for Southern Africa and in 1999 became Chief Photographer for Eastern and Southern Africa in Nairobi.

### Nidal al-Mughrabi

Mughrabi has worked for Reuters in the Gaza Strip since 1996, covering all the major events there in recent times, including the Palestinian uprising.

### Ammar Awad

Awad worked for AFP in Jerusalem from 1998 to 2000, then moved to AP for a couple of months. He started working for Reuters in May 2000. Having been injured several times during the course of his work since then, Awad says he remains committed to covering the conflict.

### Laszlo Balogh

Born in Budapest in 1958, Balogh started his career as a photographer in 1975 at a Hungarian national daily newspaper and joined Reuters in 1989, right after sweeping political changes started in the country. In the past 13 years, he has covered a number of major events including the Balkans wars.

### Gary A. Cameron

Gary A. Cameron received his B.A. in Photojournalism and History from San Francisco State University. After 10 years as staff photographer with the *Washington Post,* he joined Reuters in 1990 and covered the White House till 1998. He shot the Winter Olympics ice hockey in Salt Lake City in 2002.

### Yannis Behrakis

Yannis Behrakis was born in Athens in 1960 and has worked for Reuters since 1987. He has covered wars in the former Yugoslavia and in Chechnya as well as stories in Asia, Africa, the Middle East and Eastern Europe. He has won numerous photo awards.

### Ninian Carter

Carter has been with Reuters News Graphics Service for five years. He earned his degree in Graphic Design at the Heriot-Watt University, Edinburgh, and began in 1991 at the *Edinburgh Evening News.* He later worked with *The Scotsman, The Observer* and the JSI (news graphics) Agency, Paris.

### Natalie Behring

Behring was born in 1972 and received a Bachelor of Arts degree in history. She began her work with Reuters Beijing in 1997 and has since worked for Reuters in China and the Middle East. She left Reuters in February 2002 and is now living in Kabul.

### Bernd Debusmann

Debusmann has been assigned to Vienna, Belgrade, Addis Ababa, Beirut, Nairobi, Mexico City, Prague, Miami and Washington. He reported on the conflict in the Middle East, Africa and Latin America. He is now Reuters News Editor for the Americas.

### Desmond Boylan

In 1992 Boylan started working for Reuters based in Madrid, Spain. Since then he has covered major news and sporting events, traveling in Africa, the Balkans, the Middle East and Europe.

### Nir Elias

Born in 1971 in Jerusalem, Elias worked for Flash 90 agency for two years after graduating from a three-year photography course. He is currently a photojournalist for Reuters and has covered some of the major events in the Middle East.

### Alan Elsner

Born in London, Elsner emigrated to Israel in 1977. The first permanent Reuters correspondent in Jerusalem 1983–85, he was Chief Correspondent Nordic Countries (1987–89), State Department Correspondent (1989–94), Chief U.S. Political Correspondent (1994–2000) and U.S. National Correspondent (2000–present).

### Howard Goller

Deputy Editor of the Reuters World Desk in London, Goller reported on war and peace for 18 years from the Israeli-Palestinian front line where he was Reuters Deputy Bureau Chief and headed the Foreign Press Association. Educated at Northwestern University and Yale Law School, Goller also teaches journalism.

### Michele Gershberg

Gershberg has been a correspondent with Reuters Jerusalem Bureau for the past two years covering the Israeli-Palestinian conflict. She has also worked as an economic correspondent, writing about Israel's high-tech sector.

### Rula Halawani

Rula Halawani, a freelance photographer, received a Master's degree in Photographic Studies from the University of Westminster in London in 2001. She worked two stints for Reuters in the 1990s and is a professor of photography at the Birzeit University in the West Bank.

### Megan Goldin

Goldin has covered Israel, the West Bank and Gaza Strip for six years for Reuters and as a television producer and radio reporter for the Australian Broadcasting Corporation's Middle East bureau.

### Nayef Hashlamoun

Hashlamoun is a Birzeit University graduate student in International Studies. He has certificates of recognition from the Arab Journalist Association and the Palestinian Council for Culture and Journalism. He is director of AL-WATAN Center and President of UNESCO Club in Hebron.

### Christine Hauser

Hauser, based in Jerusalem, reported for UPI during the 1991 Gulf War. She has reported for Reuters in the Middle East since 1992, including assignments in Iraq, Libya, Chad, Sudan and Afghanistan. She has a Master's Degree in Middle Eastern Languages and Cultures from Columbia University.

### Timothy Heritage

Heritage has been Jerusalem Bureau Chief since July 2000. In earlier assignments in Moscow, Warsaw, Belgrade and Brussels, Heritage covered events including "perestroika," Solidarity's rise to power and the Balkans conflicts.

### Loay Abu Haykel

Abu Haykel has worked for four years covering events in the city of Hebron. He started as a photographer's assistant and is a self-taught photojournalist.

### Gary Hershorn

Born in Ontario, Canada, in 1958, Hershorn worked at United Press Canada until 1985, when Reuters hired him as Chief Photographer for Canada in Toronto. In 1990 he transferred to his current base, Washington, where he works as Editor Pictures, Americas.

### Jeffrey Heller

Heller, 47, Editor-in-Charge in the Reuters Jerusalem bureau, has been covering the Middle East since 1980. Born in New York, he moved to Israel as a teenager. From 1987 to 1993 he reported for Reuters from London and worked on the Middle East and Africa Editing Desk in Nicosia, Cyprus.

### Evelyn Hockstein

Evelyn Hockstein, an American freelance photojournalist, has covered the Israeli-Palestinian conflict for Reuters, the *Philadelphia Inquirer,* and Knight Ridder/Tribune. She has been a Pew Fellow in International Journalism at Johns Hopkins School of Advanced International Studies in Washington.

### Jim Hollander

After covering the 1982 war in Lebanon, Hollander transferred to Tel Aviv as UPI Chief Photographer. In 1985 he joined Reuters where he has covered events in Israel, the Occupied Territories and the Palestinian Authority areas. He recently covered the conflict in and around Afghanistan. He is a Senior Photographer based in Jerusalem.

### Ahmed Jadallah

Born in Gaza in 1970, Jadallah has been with Reuters since 1992. He received a degree in science from Gaza University and one in public relations and media from Al Azhar University in Gaza. Jadallah has exhibited in Europe and the Middle East and won first prize at the Dubai Press Club in 2002.

### Paul Holmes

Paul Holmes was the Reuters Bureau Chief in Jerusalem from 1997 to 2000. A Briton now based in Paris, he has reported for Reuters from some 40 countries including Iraq, Jordan, Lebanon, Egypt and Saudi Arabia.

### Stephen Jaffe

Stephen Jaffe is based in Washington and worked for Agence France Presse for five years. He has covered the White House for 12 years as well as many major news events and has won a number of high-profile photography awards.

### Majed Jaber

Jaber, 52, started working with UPI in 1980, then moved to Reuters in 1985. He has covered major events ranging from the movement of Palestinian refugees to Jordan during the 1967 Israel-Arab war to the 1990 Madrid Peace Conference.

### Ali Jarekji

Jarekji, a 48-year-old Syrian, started working with Reuters in 1985. He covered the Lebanon war, working for UPI and AP. Since 1992 he has worked out of Jordan.

### Magnus Johansson

Born in 1972 in Sweden, Johansson covered the fall of communism in former Eastern Europe and the collapse of apartheid in South Africa. A contract with Pressens Bild in Stockholm in 1998 took him to Israel to cover the Palestinian uprising. In August 2001 he joined the Reuters team in Jerusalem.

### Barbara Kinney

For six years until April 1999, Kinney was a personal photographer for President Clinton. Her photos appeared on the covers of *Time* and *Newsweek*. Earlier, 1982–88, she was a picture editor and photographer for *USA Today*. Recently she has been Reuters Global Entertainment Picture Editor.

### Havakuk Levison

Born in Zutphen, the Netherlands, in 1942, Levison studied photography in Rotterdam and in 1968 became a press photographer for Newspot in Israel. He worked at the *Israel Sun* and in 1971 started as a freelance photographer, working for AP and UPI. Since 1985 he has covered major events for Reuters.

### Reinhard Krause

Born in 1959, Krause became a photographer in 1979 and joined Reuters in 1989 during the fall of the Berlin Wall. Since February 2001 he has been Chief Photographer Israel and the Palestinian Territories.

### Alistair Lyon

Alistair Lyon, Reuters Middle East diplomatic correspondent, spent 27 years in the region, joining Reuters in Lebanon in 1984 and heading bureaus in Jordan, Turkey, Pakistan and Egypt before moving to London in 2001.

### Kevin Lamarque

Lamarque has been with Reuters for 15 years, spending two years in Hong Kong (1987–89) before transferring to London (1989–99), where he covered everything from the troubles in Northern Ireland to the funeral of the Princess of Wales. He is now based in Washington covering the White House.

### Gil Cohen Magen

Born in 1971, Magen studied photography at Hadassa College, Jerusalem. In 1999 he became a photojournalist for a local newspaper in Israel. He then started work with Reuters. He has staged several photography exhibitions.

### Jerry Lampen

Jerry Lampen, born in Rotterdam in 1961, became a news and sports photographer at a Rotterdam agency in 1981. In 1985 he joined United Photos in Haarlem, returning in 1987 to Rotterdam, where he worked with picture agencies and began covering sports and general news for Reuters.

### Robert Mahoney

Robert Mahoney, Reuters Jerusalem Bureau Chief 1990–97, covered the Palestinian uprising, the Gulf War, the Oslo Accords and the Yitzhak Rabin assassination and its aftermath. He has been a correspondent in Asia, Africa and Europe and is now in charge of Reuters World Desk in London.

### Moshe Milner

From 1967–79 Milner worked for the Israeli Government Press Office and from 1979–90 he was a photographer for Sygma in Israel. His photos have appeared in such magazines as *Time*, *Newsweek*, *Life*, *Paris Match* and *Stern*. He is photo editor of the Israeli National Photo Archives.

### Patrick Massey

Massey covered the Six-Day War in 1967, the Jordan Civil War in 1970 and after that Northern Ireland, Cyprus and the fall of Saigon. He was Chief Correspondent, Israel, from 1977–82, then spent time in Beirut covering the Israeli invasion. From 1983–86 he was Chief Correspondent, Tokyo.

### Jason Pickersgill

Pickersgill qualified in Newspaper Design & Information Graphics at Newcastle College. Since June 2001 he has freelanced with Reuters News Graphics Service. He worked for Britain's *Independent* and *Observer* newspapers, then for BBC Sports online as a web information graphics designer.

### Win McNamee

McNamee graduated as a journalism major from the University of South Carolina in 1985. He joined Reuters in 1990 as a staff photographer in Washington. He has covered four U.S. presidents and the Gulf War, as well as conflicts in the Philippines, South Korea and Afghanistan.

### Oleg Popov

Popov has been a photographer for the Bulgarian Telegraph Agency and for *Sport Weekly Magazine* and *Narodna Mladezh*, a Bulgarian daily. He began working for Reuters in 1990 and became a staff photographer in 1994. He has covered wars in the Balkans and in Chechnya, and many sporting events.

### Abed Omar Qusini

Born in Nablus in 1967, Abed Omar Qusini studied the English language before becoming a Reuters photographer in 1998.

### David Rogers

Rogers joined Reuters in 1967 and retired in 2000 as Chief News Editor. He reported from China, South Africa and the Middle East and witnessed the assassination of Anwar Sadat. He reported the 1973 Middle East war and the 1982 Lebanon invasion and was Middle East Editor for the Gulf War.

### Radu Sigheti

Born in Bucharest in 1959, Sigheti worked at the photo studio of Romania's biggest printing house from 1980 to 1989 and spent 10 months working for *Romania*, a monthly magazine published for embassies abroad. He joined Reuters in October 1990.

### Larry Rubenstein

In 1987 Rubenstein joined Reuters as Chief Photographer and then became Assistant Picture Editor. In June 2000 he became Editorial Logistics Manager, Text, Pictures and Television. He has photographed Presidents Carter, Reagan, Bush, Clinton and Bush and won several awards.

### David Silverman

Silverman was born in Johannesburg in 1962, emigrating to Israel in 1983. He studied at the Camera Obscura visual arts college in Jerusalem and Tel Aviv and served for two years as an Israeli army photographer. In 1991 he began work for Reuters in Jerusalem, leaving in 1999 to join his family in England.

### Damir Sagolj

Born in Sarajevo in 1971, Sagolj worked with the Paris-based Sipa press agency for several years before joining Reuters in 1996 as a Bosnia photographer.

### Osama Silwadi

Silwadi, a Palestinian photojournalist, was born in Ramallah in 1973. He earned his Media Telecommunications degree in 1991. He has shown his photography in Rome, Cairo and the United States. In 1993 Silwadi became a journalist and in 1998 he started work for Reuters in the West Bank.

### Suhaib Salem

Having studied journalism and media, Salem has worked with Reuters as a photojournalist since 1997. He won a prize in the 2000 world press photography competition.

### Matt Spetalnick

Joining Reuters in 1983, Spetalnick has covered Latin American coups and drug wars, the Kosovo crisis and the Iran-Iraq war, the 1992 Los Angeles riots, the O.J. Simpson case and the Basque separatist conflict. In 2001 he became Reuters Deputy Bureau Chief for Israel and the Palestinian territories.

### Mike Tyler

A freelancer for Reuters News Graphics in London since 1997, Tyler studied graphic design at John Moores University, Liverpool. He worked on a range of corporate identity projects before establishing Mapstyle, a custom map design service, in 1994.

### Paul Taylor

Taylor is Reuters European Affairs Editor based in Brussels. He was bureau chief in Jerusalem from 1986–90, covering the first Palestinian uprising, and as Diplomatic Editor in 1997–2001 he helped to cover the 2000 Camp David Peace Summit.

### Rick Wilking

Born in Madison, Wisconsin, in 1955, Wilking began as a photographer with UPI in Denver, Colorado. He became UPI's Chief Photographer, Switzerland, in 1983. He joined Reuters in 1985 and was made Senior Photographer in Washington in 1989. In 1998 Wilking returned to Denver as a freelancer.

### Goran Tomasevic

Goran Tomasevic joined the oldest newspaper in the Balkans, *Politika*, in 1991. He started working for Reuters as a freelance photographer in 1996 and says his greatest career challenge was covering the conflict in Kosovo.

### Jonathan Wright

Wright, a foreign affairs correspondent in Washington, joined Reuters in Cairo in 1980 and was present at the assassination of President Anwar Sadat in 1981. He has since worked in Beirut, London, the Gulf, Nairobi, Tunis and Nicosia.

Additional pictures by **Amit Shabi**.